LONDON UNDE
ROLLING STO

Capital Transport

Frontispiece:
An eastbound train of 1992 Tube Stock arrives at East Acton on the Central Line in April 2002, with DM 91137 leading. This station still retains much of its 'halt' type character from when opened in 1920.
Brian Hardy

ABBREVIATIONS

Abbreviations used for Carbuilders:

ABB	ABB Transportation (later ADtranz), Derby. Now Bombardier Transportation.
BREL	BREL Ltd, Derby (later became ABB Transportation Ltd).
Birmingham	Birmingham Railway Carriage & Wagon Company Ltd.
Bombardier	Bombardier Prorail Ltd, Horbury, Wakefield. Now Bombardier Transportation.
Cravens	Cravens Ltd, Sheffield.
Derby	British Railways Workshops, Derby.
Gloucester	Gloucester Railway Carriage & Wagon Company Ltd.
Metro-Cammell	Metropolitan-Cammell Carriage & Wagon Company Ltd, Birmingham. Now Alstom.
RFS	RFS Industries, Doncaster. Now Bombardier Transportation.

Other Abbreviations used:

ATO	Automatic Train Operation
ATP	Automatic Train Protection
BRML	British Rail Maintenance Ltd
CDU	Cab Display Unit
CSDE	Correct Side Door Enable
CCTV	Closed Circuit Television
DVA	Digitised Voice Announcer
ETT	Experimental Tube Train
ERU	Emergency Response Unit
GEC	General Electric Company
JLE	Jubilee Line Extension
LT	London Transport
LUL	London Underground Limited
NSE	Network SouthEast
OPO	One-person operation
PLS	Programme Logic System
PPP	Public Private Partnership
SCAT	Speed Control After Tripping
TEP	Train Equipment Panel
TMS	Train Monitoring System

Fifteenth edition 2002

ISBN 185414 263 1

Published by
Capital Transport Publishing,
38 Long Elmes,
Harrow Weald, Middlesex

Designed by Tim Demuth

Printed by CS Graphics,
Singapore

CONTENTS

AUTHOR'S NOTE

This 15th edition of London Underground Rolling Stock describes and illustrates the rolling stock on London's Underground, along with other operators with relevant 'London' connections.

In the five years since the last edition of this book, much has changed. The Jubilee Line Extension opened in stages in 1999 and the 1996 Tube Stock has all entered service, replacing the 1983 Tube Stock on the original section of the Jubilee Line, the last of which is now being disposed of. Similar in appearance to the 1996 Stock is the 1995 Tube Stock on the Northern Line, which replaced all the 1956/59/62 and 1972 MkI Tube Stock. Train refurbishment programmes have been completed on the Piccadilly Line (1973 Tube Stock) and on the Metropolitan Line (A60/62 Stock) – the latter stock also works on the East London Line, which reopened in March 1998 after a three-year closure for complete line refurbishment. More recently, a trial refurbishment on a trailer car of District Line D Stock has been completed, pending authorisation of fleet refurbishment – the D Stock is now the last unrefurbished and unpainted stock on the Underground.

Other changes have seen a fleet-wide introduction of inter-car barriers on all trains (provided new on 1995/96 Stock) and, apart from the Victoria Line, adoption of 'Correct Side Door Enable' (CSDE), preventing train operators opening the doors on the wrong side at stations. Many engineering modifications (some visible and some audible) have also been undertaken on various stocks.

After much discussion and political wrangling, it was announced on 7 February 2002 that the Public Private Partnership (PPP) of the

Inter-car barriers have been fitted to all stocks since the last edition of this book. The inter-car barriers on stocks prior to 1995 comprise fittings on car ends, between which is attached a plastic-type 'curtain' to prevent passengers falling between carriages. 1995 and 1996 Stocks were fitted with solid rubber barriers from new. The arrangement between 1972 MkII Tube Stock is seen at Kensal Green in May 2002. Similar arrangements are in use on surface stock, as seen between A Stock DMs (single-ended DM 5152 left and double-ended unit DM 5099 right) at Farringdon in April 2002.
Brian Hardy

New trains are to be built by Bombardier for the Metronet Consortium for use on the Victoria Line. They are due to be introduced between 2008 and 2010.

Underground would proceed. The net result will see an enormous amount of cash being invested in the Underground, updating signalling, stations and track, and building new trains. The first recipient of new trains is likely to be the Victoria Line, followed by the Metropolitan Line. The latter's A60/62 Stock is now 40 years old.

This book is not an official publication of London Underground Limited and opinions expressed are thus those of the author. Thanks are given to those who have contributed and offered advice, especially to engineering and depot staff of the three Infracos (BCV, JNP and SSL), London's Transport Museum, photographic contributors and many others. Thanks are given to my wife Jeanne for assisting with the typing and checking the typescript. Tony Morgan kindly assisted with checking of the typescript and the numerical data.

The London Underground Railway Society publishes regular rolling stock information in its monthly magazine 'Underground News', to enable its members to keep the information in this book up to date. Details of membership can be obtained by post from the Hon. Secretary at 54 Brinkley Road, Worcester Park, Surrey, KT4 8JF.

The information in this book is correct to 1 July 2002.

London Underground Ltd operates two main types of passenger rolling stock on its railways. One is known as surface stock and is built to full-size gauge for use on the Metropolitan, Circle, Hammersmith & City, District and East London lines, whose tunnel sections are double-tracked and built just below surface level. The other type, tube stock, is used on the Bakerloo, Piccadilly, Northern, Jubilee, Central, Victoria and Waterloo & City lines, which have deep-level single track tunnels of about 12ft diameter. The tube tunnels on the Jubilee Line extension east of Green Park, however, have been built to a diameter of 14ft.

In the case of tube stock, the different groups are distinguished by the year of anticipated delivery at the time of ordering. Surface stock is distinguished by letters and the last two digits of the year of anticipated delivery. The District Line stock, officially known as D Stock, was originally designated D78 Stock.

Each train is composed of one or more units coupled together as necessary to form trains of the required length. Units are formed of a number of motor cars and trailer cars semi-permanently coupled. Each unit is self-sufficient as regards current supply for motors,

The sharp curve of the Bakerloo Line platforms at Waterloo are evident here as a northbound train is seen departing.
Capital Transport

lighting, compressed air supply and auxiliary equipment. Some stocks have units which cannot be operated in service on their own, as they have a driver's cab at one end only, with a shunting control panel at the other. The Central Line's 1992 Tube Stock also has some units which have a shunting control panel at each end and therefore these will always be formed in the middle of trains.

The different types of car are:

DM Driving Motor car, having traction motors and a driver's cab.

NDM Non-Driving Motor car – as DM but without a driver's cab.

UNDM Uncoupling Non-Driving Motor car – as NDM but provided with control cabinet at one end to allow uncoupling and shunting of a unit without loss of space incurred by cab.

T Trailer car – without motors or cab.

To assist in identification, the end cars of units are referred to as 'A' cars (which normally face north or west) or 'D' cars (south or east). Car numbering is also arranged so that distinction can not only be made between 'A' and 'D' cars but also between the types of car and stock. To simplify shunting operations in Stonebridge Park depot, the arrangements on the Bakerloo Line are opposite to that just described. It should be noted, however, that on lines that have loops at terminal stations (Kennington on the Northern Line and Heathrow on the Piccadilly Line) or have triangular junction layouts (for example Rickmansworth – Croxley – Moor Park on the Metropolitan Line), trains will become turned and may face the opposite direction to that mentioned above. The trains on the Central Line, however, are fully reversible and are not identified with the 'A' and 'D' nomenclature. A similar principle has been applied to the Northern Line's 1995 Tube Stock.

Over the period, 1984–2000, all trains on the Underground have become one-person operated. The majority of OPO rolling stock have been 'conversions' of existing crew-operated trains and only the 1992, 1995 and 1996 Tube Stocks have been one-person operated from new.

The line allocations of the different types of stock, including spares, are as shown below as at 1 July 2002.

Underground line	Train type	Train length	Quantity
Bakerloo Line	1972 MkII Stock	7-car trains	36 trains *
Jubilee Line	1996 Stock	6-car trains	59 trains ‡
Central Line	1992 Stock	8-car trains	85 trains ‡
Waterloo & City Line	1992 Stock	4-car trains	5 trains
Northern Line	1995 Stock	6-car trains	106 trains
Piccadilly Line	1973 Stock	6-car trains	86½ trains ‡
Victoria Line	1967 Stock	8-car trains	43 trains *
District Line	C69/77 Stock	6-car trains	11 trains §
	D Stock	6-car trains	75 trains ‡
H&C and Circle lines	C69/77 Stock	6-car trains	35 trains ‡
Metropolitan Line	A60/62 Stock	8-car trains †	56½ trains

* Includes some cars of 1972 MkI Tube Stock.

† Single 4-car units operate on the Chesham shuttle and on the East London Line, the latter being part of the Metropolitan Line allocation.

‡ Includes damaged stock extant.

§ Edgware Road – Olympia / Wimbledon section.

1967 TUBE STOCK

A southbound Victoria Line train of 1967 Tube Stock arrives at Stockwell on 18 August 2001. Note that a grab rail (and step plate) has been fitted to these trains on one side only, for crew relief purposes (at Seven Sisters), to avoid the train operator struggling through a potentially crowded saloon. Crew reliefs would not normally take place on the opposite side on the Victoria Line.
Daniel Woodhouse

The 1967 Tube Stock is now the oldest 'tube' type rolling stock in passenger service on the London Underground. The stock was the result of successful trials with converted 1960 Tube Stock for Automatic Train Operation (ATO) on the 3.8-mile Central Line branch between Hainault and Woodford from 5 April 1964, following which it was decided that the Victoria Line should be operated with automatic trains from its opening. The system would be very similar to that used on the Central Line between Hainault and Woodford but with some improvements.

The stock for the Victoria Line was built by Metro-Cammell and was formed into four-car units (M-T-T-M), two such units being required for each train. The double-width car windows and 'pull down' ventilators were features carried on from the prototype 1960 stock motor cars. The passenger door windows were extended upwards to improve the vision for standing passengers, an idea tried out on 1938 Stock car DM 10306 back in 1949 but not incorporated until 1967. For the train operator, maximum vision was achieved by the provision of curved-round cab windows. This was a later feature, for earlier design proposals envisaged a 1962 stock style cab front, but with modifications.

Draught screen positions were set back from the door openings and the interior seating on DM cars was reduced in consequence to 40 passengers. Trailer cars were built from new with longitudinal seats in the centre bay instead of transverse ones, providing a greater standing area, but reducing the seating capacity further to 36. Powerful headlights were provided on the driving motor cars, one on each side of the front cab door and in addition to the twin red tail lights a stabling light was fitted. Illuminated advertisement panels were provided in all cars when new. By then a standard feature, external door indicator lights were provided.

A combined 'traction/brake controller' was provided in the driving cab, taking the place of separate equipment for motoring and braking, with all such positions being provided on one handle. A hydraulic handbrake, one of which was capable of holding a loaded train on the steepest gradient, was provided in each cab. These have now been replaced by spring applied parking brakes. Because of the additional equipment provided on this stock (for ATO and for rheostatic braking), the motor alternator was located on the trailer cars. A 'vigilance' button was provided for manual driving.

Other innovations included public address equipment, a 'carrier wave' communication system whereby the train operator spoke directly to the signal operator (then called 'Regulator') in Cobourg Street (Euston) control room (since superseded by train radio), a yellow 'calling on' light that can be illuminated to call a following train on for assistance, and communication between cabs on the train enabling the operator to speak to station staff at the rear of the train should the need arise.

The contract for the 1967 Stock was placed in March 1964 and the original order was for 30½ 8-car trains, comprising 122 driving motor cars (61 'A' end north cars 3001–3061 and 61 'D' end south cars 3101–3161) and 122 trailers (4001–4061 and 4101–4161) to operate between Walthamstow and Victoria. The first 4-car unit was delivered to Ruislip depot on 27 September 1967. When the extension south from Victoria to Brixton was authorised, an additional nine trains, comprising 36 motor cars (3062–3079 and 3162–3179) and 36 trailers (4062–4079 and 4162–4179) were ordered from Metro-Cammell, identical to the first batch, which made a total of 39½ trains in all.

After being delivered to Ruislip depot for commissioning, most units of 1967 stock were transferred to Hainault depot for ATO trials between Hainault and Woodford in single 4-car formations. The first to enter passenger service was unit 3009 on 21 February 1968. After these trials they were transferred to the Victoria Line depot at Northumberland Park for storage until the new line became operational. The first train, comprising units 3009 and 3011, arrived

At Oxford Circus, a northbound train of 1967 Tube Stock arrives, showing not only the recently-fitted grab rail, but also the step plate in the raised position. Automatic driving on this line means that the train operator does not have to be in the conventional driving position, because an emergency brake is provided on the opposite side. Leading is a DM of a double-ended unit, recognisable by having inter-car-barrier fittings at the car corners.
Capital Transport

on 1 April 1968. Enough trains had reached Northumberland Park to operate the first stage of the new line, which was opened between Highbury & Islington and Walthamstow Central on 1 September 1968.

Even after the Victoria Line had opened, at least one unit of 1967 Tube Stock (sometimes more) could be found on the Hainault – Woodford shuttle service on the Central Line, initially covering for 1960 Stock overhauls and latterly during the conversion of 1938 Stock trailers which replaced Pre-1938 trailers. However, 1967 Stock units were changed over between Hainault and Northumberland Park depots periodically for maintenance. From 1984 the 1967 stock was no longer required on the Central Line, and the last unit returned to the Victoria Line in May of that year.

The dramatic increase in passenger traffic in the mid-1980s required London Underground to consider additional trains for the Victoria Line service. Plans were drawn up to create an additional seven 4-car units by converting some units of 1972 MkI Stock from the Northern Line. This was done at Acton Works between 1987 and 1989. The additional units are single-ended, the 1972 cars being formed in the middle of 8-car trains. The work not only involved the renumbering of the 1972 converted cars, but also some of the 1967 stock cars involved with the scheme, which gave 32 'A' end, 32 'D' end and 22 double-ended 4-car units, making a line total of 43 8-car trains, 3½ more than hitherto. Two motor-trailer pairs were also converted from 'D' cars to 'A' cars and those involved can be found in the renumbering section later in this book.

An interior view of a Victoria Line 1967 Tube Stock DM, after some ten years of wear in refurbished condition. DM cars have transverse seats in the centre bay. On refurbishment these trains were fitted with dummy fans.
Capital Transport

During 1989 and into early 1990 all 43 Victoria Line trains were modified at Acton Works by having 'passenger alarm' push buttons fitted, along with improved safety features. A new spring-applied parking brake replaced the original hydraulic handbrake. Two units so modified (3061 and 3110) were selected for refurbishment trials, this being done in 1989 by Vic Berry of Leicester and Tickford Rail. The interiors were completely gutted and new lighting, seating, flooring, stylish panelling and grab rails were fitted. The exteriors were painted in a livery of blue above the waist, white below, red front cabs and grey roofs. The train re-entered service on 9 October 1989. It was subsequently decided that the whole Victoria Line fleet of 43 trains should be refurbished, the first train (comprising units 3005 and 3185) being despatched in June 1990. The work was undertaken by Tickford Rail Ltd at Rosyth Royal Dockyard. The exteriors were painted in what had become the new corporate 'red doors' livery – off white with a blue skirt, red cab ends and grey roofs. Only operative cabs were given red-painted ends. Cabs relegated to the middle of trains (on single-ended units) had the blue and white (with grey cab door) extended around the middle cab area. Inside, the finished product is similar to the prototype, with refinements, and include space for fans to be fitted at a later date. Passenger alarm push-buttons have been replaced by handles and an audible door-close bleep has been provided. The Victoria Line light blue colour has been used on grab rails. In the driving cab, improvements have also been made and the old lever-operated door controls have been replaced by push buttons.

Interior of 1967 Tube Stock trailer 4177, showing that the centre bay has longitudinal seating. Note also that later refurbished units (and the earlier ones since overhaul) have the seat tops covered in a blue material. Victoria Line blue dominates the car interior on the grab poles, armrests, flooring by the doorway areas, and on some other fittings. Capital Transport

The refurbishment programme was completed in May 1995. The last train, comprising units 3016+3186, was finished with different features. The trailing ends of all cars were painted dark grey to improve the between cars appearance. Unit 3186 was modified to provide additional standing space, in that the former double transverse seats were reduced to 'generous sized' single seats, while in the trailer cars, the four seats in the centre section next to the doorways were replaced by 'perch seats'. In the case of the latter, the interior windows were reduced by half but the exterior windows remained the same, although blacked out where they could not be seen through. Unit 3016 in fact comprises two cars of 1972 MkI Stock (ex-3204 and 4204) which have been converted from 'A' to 'D' cars and renumbered 3116 and 4116 respectively. The original 3116 and 4116 have been converted from 'D' to 'A' cars and renumbered 3016 and 4016, replacing collision damaged cars of the same numbers. The original 4016 has been scrapped, while the original 3016 was purchased for preservation.

Driving motor car 3184 was damaged in a collision in Northumberland Park depot on 22 February 1997. Its place has been taken by DM 3156 which, although the middle DM in a single-ended unit, could easily be converted to an outer end DM. Therefore, DM 3184 was replaced by 3156 (suitably renumbered 3184 in May 1999) and DM 3156 was replaced by 1972 MkI DM car 3312, which was renumbered to 3156 at the same time. The original 3184 was eventually scrapped in July 2000.

The current fleet of 1967 Tube Stock on the Victoria Line comprises forty-three 8-car trains, which include some cars of 1972 MkI Tube Stock, summarised as follows:

		1967	1972 MkI	Total
DM	30xx	79	7	86
T	40xx	79	7	86
T	41xx	78	8	86
DM	31xx	77	9	86
		313	31	344

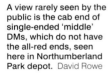

A view rarely seen by the public is the cab end of single-ended 'middle' DMs, which do not have the all-red ends, seen here in Northumberland Park depot. David Rowe

1972 TUBE STOCK

The 1972 MkII Tube Stock operates on the Bakerloo Line and shares Railtrack metals north of Queen's Park. A 7-car train arrives at Kensal Green in May 2002. Leading is 'A'-end DM 3243, which was the last train (with unit 3534) of this stock to enter service on the Bakerloo Line, some 4–5 years after the majority had begun life on the Northern Line.
Brian Hardy

The 1972 Tube Stock was almost identical in design to the Victoria Line's 1967 Stock, but was built for crew operation. This group of rolling stock came about because of the deteriorating condition of the 1938 Tube Stock on the Northern Line – a damaging strike by craftsmen at Acton Works in 1969 had led to the cancellation of many trains because of equipment problems, mostly affecting compressors. Politics therefore played a substantial part in ordering thirty 7-car trains for the Northern Line. This became the 1972 MkI Tube Stock and was built by Metro-Cammell. The trains were formed into 3- and 4-car units, one of each being required for each train (M-T-T-M+ UNDM-T-M). The shunting control equipment for the new UNDM cars was obtained from withdrawn 1938/49 stock UNDM cars.

What turned out to be the first order comprised 90 driving motor cars, 90 trailers and 30 uncoupling non-driving motor cars, all in unpainted aluminium. The stock was numbered 3201–3230 ('A' end DMs), 3301–3330 ('D' end DMs), 3501–3530 ('D' end DMs with mechanical couplers only), 4201–4230, 4301–4330 and 4501–4530 (trailers) and 3401–3430 (UNDMs). External door-indicator lights were fitted, now a standard item on new stock. The first train entered service on the Northern Line on 26 June 1972 (units 3202 and 3502) and all 30 were in service by June 1973.

As will be seen below, some of these cars were later converted to run on the Victoria Line, while others were converted to one-person operation for the Bakerloo Line. However, the Northern Line's MkI

The Bakerloo Line's fleet comprises some cars of 1972 MkI Tube Stock converted to work with the main fleet. 'D'-end DM 3566 (originally MkI DM 3524) heads a northbound train between South Kenton and Kenton. To simplify shunting operations with UNDM cars in Stonebridge Park depot, all Bakerloo Line trains operate 'A'-end south and 'D'-end north. Fred Ivey

fleet remained at twenty 7-car trains at the time when the 1995 Tube Stock began to enter service, from when withdrawals began. The last train of 1972 MkI Tube Stock was withdrawn from passenger service on 3 February 1999 (units 3227+3518).

A number of plans were put forward for the future use of the 1972 MkI Tube Stock once it was displaced, but in the meantime it was stored at various locations around the Underground system. Those not earmarked for possible use were scrapped, the net result being that two 3-car units and nineteen 4-car units were put into store. Indeed, some cars were moved off LUL metals by road to the safe confines of DERA at Shoeburyness.

Such plans included four additional 8-car trains for the Victoria Line (eight units), five units for the Waterloo & City Line (to replace the Network SouthEast liveried 1992 Stock, which would then boost the Central Line's fleet) and the remainder for pilot duties and spares. At the time of writing, all the stored units remain intact, but with little prospect of being used again.

The second batch of 1972 Tube Stock (the 1972 MkII) was also the result of politics dominating London's transport scene. A lack of rolling stock orders at Metro-Cammell led to more trains being ordered rather than allowing the company to 'fold'. It so happened that new trains were required for the first stage of the Fleet Line. This was not expected to open until the Queen's Silver Jubilee in 1977 – in the end it did not open until 1979! – so the trains were first able to enter service on the Northern Line (further improving matters by replacing more 1938 Tube Stock on what had become tagged the *Misery Line*). The trains would then go to the Jubilee Line, which by then had been renamed from the Fleet Line.

The 1972 MkII order for 33 trains continued in service longer than the MkI Stock. The fleet has been boosted in more recent years by the adaptation and conversion of some MkI cars, of which more below. The order for the 1972 MkII Stock was also placed with Metro-Cammell and comprised 99 driving motor cars, 99 trailers and 33 uncoupling non-driving motor cars. The MkII Stock was numbered 3231–3263 ('A' end DMs), 3331–3363 ('D' end DMs), 3531–3563 ('D' end DMs with mechanical couplers only), 4231–4263, 4331–4363 and 4531–4563 (trailers) and 3431–3463 (UNDMs). The first trains of 1972 MkII Stock entered service on 19 November 1973.

Although similar in appearance to the MkI cars, red-painted passenger doors were introduced on the MkII Stock and all-red roundels replaced 'Underground' transfers on the motor car sides as well as being introduced on other cars. It was the intention with the 1972 MkII Stock for it to be converted to ATO at a later date and at first some trains were provided with a motorised destination blind and electronic train set number equipment. This was soon replaced by the standard train set number plates (in the offside cab window rather than beneath the front cab door window as on 1972 MkI Stock) and hand-operated destination blinds.

From 1977 trains of 1972 MkII Stock, displaced by the 1959 Stock on the Northern Line, began working on the Bakerloo Line in readiness for the Stanmore branch becoming the Jubilee Line (in 1979). The transfer process was a gradual one, completed in time for the

1972 MkII Tube Stock with 3547 at the rear enters the tunnel at Queen's Park. When refurbished, these trains had spaces earmarked for fans, which were eventually fitted when the 1983 Tube Stock was withdrawn from the Jubilee Line in 1998. The slots for expelled air are visible on the car roof line.
Capital Transport

opening of the Jubilee Line between Stanmore and Charing Cross on 1 May 1979. In the interim period, the 1972 MkII Stock worked on the Bakerloo Line, including to and from Watford Junction.

Following the service reductions of December 1982, four MkII trains were returned to the Northern Line during 1983 and were modified so that they were compatible with the MkI type. The first train with a combination of the two types ran on the Northern Line on 12 September 1983 (units 3210 and 3533).

With the entry into service of the 1983 Stock on the Jubilee Line, a further 14 trains of 1972 MkII Stock made their way to the Northern Line between November 1984 and November 1985. This allowed the 1938 Stock to be withdrawn from the Bakerloo Line, by transferring more trains of 1959 stock from the Northern to the Bakerloo Line.

The delivery of the 1983 (batch II) Stock for the Jubilee allowed the 1972 MkII Stock on that line to be transferred to the Bakerloo, which was achieved in March 1989. On the Bakerloo Line, the 1972 MkII Stock operates 'wrong way round', in that the 'D' ends face north and the 'A' ends face south. This is to allow shunting operations in Stonebridge Park depot to be carried out from a middle (33xx) motor car rather than from an UNDM car. OPO on the Bakerloo Line commenced on 20 November 1989 after the stock had been converted at Acton Works.

The refurbishment programme referred to in the previous chapter also included the 1972 Stock fleet. The original plan was to refurbish all of the 1967 and 1972 stocks on the Victoria, Northern and Bakerloo lines. The possibility of new rolling stock for the Northern Line meant that only three trains of 1972 MkI Stock were refurbished

The interior layout of the 1972 Tube Stock is exactly the same as on the 1967 Stock counterparts, with the UNDM cars having transverse seats as on DM cars. The interior of this 1972 MkII trailer car shows the all longitudinal seating arrangement and that refurbishment has employed the use of Bakerloo Line brown colour extensively.
Capital Transport

for service on the Northern Line. These have since been absorbed into the Bakerloo Line fleet, apart from two cars subsequently written off because of collision damage.

Prior to being sent for refurbishment, one Northern Line train of 1972 MkI Stock (units 3203 and 3501) was converted to OPO to enable the Bakerloo Line stock to be increased from 33 to 34 trains. Unit 3203 had been out of service since 1985, it then being utilised for overhaul equipment spares, while 3501 was under repair following a collision. To follow in the Bakerloo Line numbering sequence, the two units became (respectively) 3264 and 3564. The refurbishment of the Bakerloo Line's 1972 MkII Stock was completed in April 1995.

The Bakerloo Line was unfortunate in having two serious collisions in 1994, one at Harrow & Wealdstone on 29 March (which saw 3539 and 4539 subsequently scrapped) and one at Piccadilly Circus on 22 April (when cars 3249 and 4249 went for scrap). Effectively one train short, the deficiency was eventually made up by converting refurbished 1972 MkI Stock units 3218+3507 from the Northern Line to one-person operation, becoming respectively 3265+3565 in October 1994. Service increases called for one more additional train and five cars from a second Northern Line refurbished 1972 MkI train (cars 4324 and 3324 and unit 3524) became 3266+3566 in June 1995. DM 3224 and trailer 4224 had been scrapped and the two remaining cars (3324 and 4324) were 'turned' and converted into 'A'-end cars, becoming 3266 and 4266 respectively. The other two cars of the unit (4365 and 3365) came from spare MkII cars 4349 and 3349.

The remaining refurbished but crew-operated 1972 MkI train on the Northern Line succumbed to OPO conversion for the Bakerloo Line, with 3210+3512 becoming 3267+3567 in June 1997. Meanwhile, yet another collision/derailment had occurred at Piccadilly Circus on 3 December 1996. DM 3257 was subsequently scrapped. The Bakerloo Line was thus one 4-car train short and the only cars then available were the three from the recent incident (4257-4357-3357) plus UNDM 3439 from the Harrow collision of 1994. A novel and unique solution was found. A four-car unit was created by 'turning' all three cars 3357-4357-4257, with DM 3357 becoming a leading 'A'-end DM. Spare UNDM 3439 was also 'turned' and became a 'D'-end UNDM in a four-car unit. Normally on the Bakerloo Line, four-car units are formed M-T-T-M but this unit would be non-standard in the formation M-T-T-UNDM. Because the unit was substantially 'different', 3357-4357-4257-3439 became respectively 3299-4299-4399-3399 in April 1999, entering service in its new guise in July 1999.

The current fleet of 1972 Tube Stock on the Bakerloo Line comprises thirty-six 7-car trains, which are formed of the following types of cars:

		1972 MkI	1972 MkII	Total
DM	32xx	4	32	36
T	42xx	4	32	36
T	43xx	3	33	36
DM	33xx	3	32	35
UNDM	33xx	–	1	1
UNDM	34xx	4	32	36
T	45xx	4	32	36
DM	35xx	4	32	36
	Total:	26	226	252

1973 TUBE STOCK

A 1973 Tube Stock train heading for Arnos Grove enters Hammersmith station following its non-stop run from Acton Town. Capital Transport

In order to provide new stock for the Piccadilly Line specifically for the Heathrow Airport extension, orders were placed with Metro-Cammell for 87½ 6-car trains (525 cars). Newly-built trains were considered a more desirable option than retaining the existing 1956/59 Tube Stock on that line, as additional space was required for luggage, which the older trains did not have. As a result, the 1956/59 Tube Stock was transferred to the Northern Line. The order comprised 196 driving motor cars, 175 trailers and 154 uncoupling non-driving motor cars. Each car was built about six feet longer than cars of earlier stock but the total length of a 6-car train was about 17 feet shorter than a seven-car 1956/59 Stock train. This enabled the complete train to fit into the platforms at all tube stations on the line, which was necessary because the stock was subsequently converted to one-person operation, which was the intention when it was built. The first train entered service on 19 July 1975 as a passenger-carrying 'special' when the extension from Hounslow West to Hatton Cross was opened, formed of units 108 and 137. The first normal passenger working occurred on 18 August 1975, comprising units 140 and 141.

The majority of trains operate in the formation M-T-UNDM+UNDM-T-M. The driving motor cars at each end were provided with mechanical couplers only, while the UNDM cars in the middle positions were fitted with automatic couplers. In addition there were twenty-one 3-car units formed M-T-M known as 'double-cab' units, with automatic couplers on each driving motor car. The purpose of these units was to give fleet flexibility, being able to replace an 'A' or 'D' end single end unit requiring maintenance. One unit was also provided to operate the Holborn – Aldwych shuttle service which continued until its closure on 30 September 1994.

The 1973 Stock was numbered 100–253 (DMs), 854-895 (DMs with automatic couplers for double-cab units), 300–453 (UNDMs), 500–653 (trailers) and even numbers only from 654–694 (trailers used in double-cab units).

Improvements incorporated in these trains were the provision of air-operated cab doors, being operated independently from the passenger doors, and 'selective door close', which enables all except one single door and one single leaf of a double door on each car to be closed, a useful facility in bad weather at terminal stations and during prolonged station stops. After trials on a 1967 Tube Stock unit, the Westcode electro-pneumatic braking system was provided, enabling the Westinghouse air brake to be omitted. The electronic control of electrical braking (ECEB) was also trialled on a 4-car unit of the erstwhile 1960 Tube Stock. A train equipment fault-finding panel was provided in the cab for the driver to identify faults on the train. Also provided was automatic wheel-slip/slide protection and load control of acceleration and braking. The motor alternator (located on the trailer cars of 1967 and 1972 stocks) was fitted on driving motor cars (as on 1962 and earlier stock) and UNDMs.

On all 1973 Stock cars, the interior seating was arranged longitudinally at each end of the saloon, with transverse seats in the centre section bay, each type of car having seats for 44 passengers. Sliding ventilators were provided above the car windows. The train set number panel had numbers of the 'flapper' type. The driving end of each DM car was given a red painted section below the cab windows, extending around the side to meet the edge of the cab door. The intention to fit three ceiling-mounted fans on each car was hampered by design and technical difficulties and it was not until October 1977 that fans were first used. Even so they were not wholly successful. Not all cars were fitted with fans and those that did have them were subsequently decommissioned. A total of 25 single-ended 'A' units were fitted from new with de-icing equipment.

Small detail differences existed on the trains from when they were new. The first 16 units (100–115) had black roof section panels (all the others were white) and a total of 22 units (100–117, 178, 179, 202 and 203) had higher waist-level join lines than the rest of the fleet. The delays in commissioning the 1973 Stock saw several units put into store when new at the Bicester Military Railway, some were returned to Metro-Cammell at Birmingham, while some were put into store in the permanent way sidings in Ruislip depot.

The extension to serve Heathrow Airport was completed for opening on 16 December 1977, on which date Her Majesty the Queen opened the section from Hatton Cross to Heathrow Central (the latter now known as Heathrow Terminals 1,2,3).

The last two double-cab units of 1973 Stock were built for experimental purposes, cars 892-692-893 having Westinghouse equipment and 894-694-895 having GEC equipment. The two units were known as the Experimental Tube Train (ETT) and testing with unit 892 on the South Ealing test tracks commenced in 1978. Having high-tech but non-standard equipment, it was necessary for the train to be 'piloted' to and from the test tracks for which a 3-car unit of 1938 Stock (10306-012498-11247) was specially adapted, being based at Northfields depot. Unit 892 was transferred to Hainault in February 1979 for testing on the Hainault – Woodford branch and it entered occasional passenger service from 25 July 1983. Testing of unit 894 commenced in September 1980, based at Northfields. When the tests were concluded, it was decided to convert the two units to standard, as additional stock would be necessary for the extension of the Piccadilly Line to serve Heathrow Terminal 4. Unit 894 entered Acton Works for conversion in early-1984 and was transferred back to Northfields on 16 August 1985, entering service on 12 February 1986. Unit 892 followed suit, arriving at Acton Works in June 1985. It was returned to Northfields on 10 October 1986, entering service on 10 April 1987.

The inter-car barrier fittings on double-ended DMs of 1973 Tube Stock are more pronounced than other stocks – they were the first of this type to be fitted. DM 866 is at the rear of a train at South Ealing. Kim Rennie

On 1 April 1986 Their Royal Highnesses the Prince and Princess of Wales officially opened the new Terminal 4 station and buildings at Heathrow Airport, for which 1973 Stock units 864 and 195 were used, being given a special headboard and side 'Concorde' stickers, as well as a special 'Terminal 4' destination blind. Trains worked non-stop through the new station and around the new single-track loop from the new timetable on 7 April until passenger services commenced on 12 April. One-way loop workings cause trains to become 'turned' and unless an even number of trips is worked, which is impossible to guarantee with the operating complexities of the Piccadilly Line, some trains finish at the end of the day the opposite way round. As the 1973 Stock is unable to couple 'A' to 'A' and 'D' to 'D' for operational purposes, the conversion of the two ex-ETT units to work with the rest of the fleet gave additional stock to assist in over-coming the problem if a unit becomes defective.

When unit 114-514-314 was new, it was used (along with 315-515-115) for crew training at the eastern end of the Piccadilly Line, being based at Cockfosters depot. When training was completed the unit was used to provide equipment spares for other trains already in service. Trailer 514 was used for experiments with ventilation in 1982, while DM 114 replaced DM 888 badly damaged by fire near Bounds Green on 11 August 1982. DM 888 was eventually scrapped in January 1993, having languished in Northfields depot for many years – it did, however, provide a source of spares for other cars. DM 114 entered service for the first time (with 688 and 889) on 31 March 1983. This left cars 314 and 514 spare, never having entered service. Trailer 514 was acquired to become the purpose-built Track Recording Car for the Underground, being converted by BREL at Derby and completed in the spring of 1987. It was renumbered TRC666 and was painted in the red and white livery carried by its 1960 stock converted pilot motors. UNDM 314 served as a temporary canteen at Northfields in 1984/85, and after a further period of disuse was used for experiments in connection with 1973 Stock refurbish-ment. It was transferred to RFS at Doncaster on 23 June 1993 for further experiments and onwards to Bombardier at Horbury on 3 November 1994. Being surplus to requirements, it was scrapped in August 2000, along with unit 204-604-404 which had been damaged

Unlike the 1967/72 Tube Stock, whose seating layouts were unaltered on refurbishment, that on the 1973 Stock changed considerably. The transverse seats in the centre bay were replaced by longitudinal seating and perches by the doors, thereby providing greater standing and luggage space, but at the expense of six seats per car. Capital Transport

in a collision at Northfields on 12 December 1990 – it was taken by road from Ruislip to Horbury in February 1995, then with the intention of its repair being completed and then refurbished. Meanwhile, DM 114 was converted to a double-ended DM and the whole unit (114-688-889) renumbered 896-696-897 respectively in April 1993.

With the transfer of overhauling stock from Acton Works to depots, Cockfosters took on the role for the 1973 Stock, the first unit of which (315-515-115) was completed in June 1986. The first of the deep-level tube lines to be converted to one-person operation was the Piccadilly Line, operative from 31 August 1987. The 1973 Stock was converted for OPO at Northfields depot (all single-ended units and two double-cab units) and Acton Works (the remaining double-cab units) during 1986 and up to September 1987. The exterior differences included the fitting of an offside window wiper and calling-on light. (When the stock was new, a calling-on light was fitted on the driver's side of the destination blind, but was later replaced by an opening for cab ventilation). In the train operator's cab, door control buttons were provided on the console and a new operator's seat fitted. From 31 August 1987, the date of OPO introduction on the Piccadilly Line, the operation of the passenger emergency alarms was changed, so that drivers could take the train on to the next station in the event of a passenger using the alarm.

Following refurbishment trials undertaken on UNDM car 314, 3-car unit 190 was chosen for exterior painting and a complete interior refurbishment. This was done by Metro-Cammell at Birmingham and was one of the first units of 1973 Stock to have a series of engineering modifications done at Acton Works to improve service reliability. The exterior was painted in the 'red doors' corporate livery, but in a shade of red darker than hitherto. Windows were installed in the trailing ends of the cars for added passenger security, while each car was given a different layout in the centre bay, which included seats and luggage accommodation. The fitting of door-close bleeps meant that an unrefurbished unit (123) had to be modified to work with it, the train entering service on 20 January 1991. For a time, DM 190 also had a black-on-yellow dot matrix destination display.

During 1992 and 1993, Correct Side Door Enable (CSDE) equipment was fitted to 1973 Stock trains and was introduced from 6 September 1993. Following this modification, the original Train Equipment fault finding panels (TEPs) were replaced with more simple Cab Display Units (CDUs), which was completed in September 1994.

The contract for refurbishing the 1973 Stock was awarded to RFS of Doncaster and the first two units (866 and 151) were taken from Ruislip depot by road in May 1993. With RFS being absorbed by Bombardier Prorail, the train was taken to Bombardier's Horbury site during November and December 1994. The exteriors have been painted in Corporate livery, but the cab is grey around and beneath the cab windows to the top of the headlights. The train set number is now incorporated above the destination area on the cab fronts. On either side of the front cab door, grab rails are provided in connection with detrainment steps, which are normally folded away under the front cab floor. Lighting is provided above the driver's side cab window and additional lighting at solebar level for use in emergencies. During refurbishment, all seating became longitudinal, reducing capacity from 44 to 38 per car. However, perch seats are provided at the car ends and by the door area in the centre bay, greatly enhancing luggage and standing space. Interior dot matrix indicators are provided and pre-set digital voice announcements are available, set up by the train operator.

The first refurbished train returned to London Underground on 7 March 1996 and re-entered service on the Piccadilly Line on 17 June 1996. The prototype refurbished unit 190 (with its partner 123) went for refurbishment as train 10 on 3 September 1996.

The refurbishment programme continued for four years, when the last unit of all (894) was sent away on 26 September 2000. (However, the last unrefurbished train of 1973 Stock to run on the Piccadilly Line did so on 20 August 2000 and comprised units 860+201, which went away on 5 September 2000). Unit 894 was one of the two ex-ETT units and when converted for service on the Piccadilly Line in 1985 was equipped with Davies & Metcalfe braking, which made it sound 'different' from the rest of the fleet. Before refurbishment, the unit was converted to standard in Northfields depot. The unit returned on 7 December 2000 but did not re-enter service until 10 July 2001.

Unlike some other European transport operators, London Underground has only 'dabbled' in using complete train exteriors for advertising purposes. The first, for 'United Airlines', involved a 6-car train of 1973 Tube Stock, comprising units 196+167, and was sent for repainting at Rosyth on 26 May 1995. It returned on 18 June 1995, re-entering service the following day after a 'launch' at Heathrow. It was intended to keep it in service on the Heathrow branch but operational reasons ensured its occasional visit to Rayners Lane and Uxbridge. It also made an unscheduled trip to Ealing Broadway (District Line) on 21 June 1995 to fill a large gap in that line's Ealing service. The train was also given new 'United Airlines' seating moquette in August 1995. It ran in this condition until October 1998, when it was despatched (as train 49) for refurbishment.

The Piccadilly Line fleet now comprises 519 cars out of an original total of 525. Five have been scrapped as noted above (DMs 204 and 888, trailer 604 and UNDMs 314 and 404), while trailer 514 is now a track recording car in the engineers train fleet.

1992 TUBE STOCK

The Central Line operates in ATO mode, only the second Underground line to be worked in this way. A westbound train arrives at Theydon Bois on 30 March 2002.
Brian Hardy

The replacement rolling stock for the Central Line was the result of extensive trials conducted with three 4-car prototype trains known as the 1986 Prototype Tube Stock. These three prototypes tested new materials and construction methods and experimented with different interior seating layouts.

Two of the 4-car prototypes were built by Metro-Cammell of Birmingham (trains 'A' and 'C'), the third (train 'B') by BREL Ltd of Derby. Electrical equipment for one of the Metro-Cammell trains was provided by GEC Traction of Manchester and for the other by Brown-Boveri of Zurich, Switzerland. Brush Electrical Machines of Loughborough provided the equipment for the BREL train. Each of the three trains was finished in a distinctive colour and to give a feeling of spaciousness and security inside, the two Metro-Cammell trains had windows in the car ends. All trains had the side windows extended up into the curve of the roof.

Each of the prototypes consisted of two 2-car motored units, one car having a driving cab and the other no cab. The automatic coupling arrangements between units and the controls of all three trains were designed to be compatible so that any combination of 2-car units could couple to form a 4-, 6- or 8-car train. The car bodies and the floor structure were constructed from wide aluminium extrusions welded together, which made them both lighter and cheaper to manufacture than tube car bodies built previously. This form of construction required external sliding doors which did not need 'pockets' in the body structure. Train 'A' was painted red, train 'B' blue and train 'C' green.

The three prototypes were delivered in 1986 and 1987 and following extensive testing, the trains operated spasmodically in passenger service from 4 May 1988 on the Jubilee Line. Their use in passenger service came to an abrupt end on 14 August 1989 when one train became derailed at Neasden. This, however, was not the sole reason for their withdrawal, for trials were scheduled to come to an end in September 1989 with a new timetable, which did not make provision for any further testing in passenger service on the Jubilee Line. The red and green trains were stored at Neasden and the blue train at Acton Works. Unloved and unwanted, 11 out of the 12 cars were scrapped between August and October 1996, while one DM from green train 'C' was acquired for preservation by London's Transport Museum.

An order for 85 trains of Central Line Replacement Stock (as it was then known – now the 1992 Tube Stock) was placed in 1989 with BREL of Derby, which became ASEA Brown Boveri (or ABB Transportation Ltd), and latterly ADtranz Ltd. It is now Bombardier Prorail. Each train of 1992 Tube Stock comprises eight cars formed of four 2-car units. There are three combinations of 2-car unit and four types of individual vehicle. Car 'A' is a driving motor with cab, shoes, traction equipment and automatic coupler. Car 'B' is a non-driving motor car having no cab or shoes, but has traction equipment which is fed from the adjacent motor car. It also has a shunting control

Interior of 1992 Tube Stock. Note that the seating in the end bays is arranged so that the centre pair are set back to increase standing room and that 'perches' are provided on either side of the communicating doors. All the armrests between seats have long since been removed.
Capital Transport

cabinet at its outer end along with an automatic coupler. Car type 'C' is similarly a non-driving motor car having no cab, but has shoes and traction equipment as an 'A' car, along with a shunting control cabinet and automatic coupler at its outer end. De-icing cars are a variation on car type 'C' and are designated as type 'D'. With these four types of car, semi-permanent 2-car units are formed as follows: 175 A-B units, 133 B-C units and 32 B-D de-icing units. All the 2-car units are fully reversible and compatible and thus there is no distinction between 'A' and 'D' ends as before. Car numbering is as follows:

Car type A	91001–91349 odd numbers
Car type B	92001–92349 odd numbers in A-B units
Car type B	92002–92266 even numbers in B-C units
Car type B	92402–92464 even numbers in B-C de-icing units
Car type C	93002–93266 even numbers in B-C units
Car type D	93402–93464 even numbers in B-D de-icing units

With the different combination of cars and units, it is possible for an 8-car train to be formed in one of 36 different ways, although DM cars are kept at the outer ends of trains whenever possible.

Each car has all longitudinal seating arranged six per side in the outer bays and five per side in the centre saloon bay (i.e. between the double doors), giving a total of 34 seats per car. The middle pair of each group of six are set back six inches to allow greater standing capacity, at which point there is a floor-to-ceiling grab pole in the centre. At non-cabbed ends (at the trailing end of car 'A' and both ends of cars 'B', 'C' and 'D') there is one perch seat in each corner position. The interior colour scheme is in soft stone, with seating moquette in warm red/ivory/blue arranged in diagonally split squares. Car floors are of rubber type material in grey/blue terrazzo chip. Grab rails are the all-round type as provided on 1986 prototype train 'A'. The large single-glazed car windows, which curve up into the roof line, have also been adopted from the prototype trains.

Passenger door control buttons were provided from new. 'Open' buttons are located in the middle of the door separations inside and out, while extra 'open' buttons are fitted inside the cars to the 'stand-back' pillars, one each side, along with door close buttons. Since early-2000, however, the train doors have been under control of the train operator on this and all stocks fitted with such equipment.

The passenger door width is 1664mm (double) and 832mm (single), each leaf being some 6 inches wider than on the prototype trains to allow speedier alighting and boarding and thereby reducing station stop times. Like the prototype trains, sliding doors are externally hung. Apart from the driving end of the 'A' cars, end windows are provided to give greater security. Other interior features include pre-programmed announcements in digitised speech. The exteriors are painted in LUL corporate livery – white, grey roof, blue skirt and red passenger doors. The cab front, although red, has the window surrounds and section immediately below it in dark grey.

The driver's cab incorporates in-cab closed circuit television, provided by Siemens/BREL, which provides pictures of the relevant station platform, including views on departure. In addition to public address, in the event of an emergency, there is two-way communication between the driver and passengers. The driver has a redesigned fore/aft traction brake controller, which is positioned on the right hand of the driver's seat – reminiscent of that provided on the 1935 streamlined tube stock!

The thyristor controlled traction equipment is provided by a consortium of ASEA Brown Boveri of Switzerland and Brush Electrical Machines of Loughborough. A computer data transmission system with multiplexing is used for much of the electrical control of the trains. This reduces the number of cables, but safety circuits such as braking are separately wired as well. The Westinghouse analogue braking system is fitted, along with air suspension. The bogies are provided by Kawasaki Heavy Industries of Osaka, Japan. Each car has six ventilation units giving full forced ventilation.

The length of each car is 16248mm over body ends, 2620mm wide over door leaves and 2869mm high at the top of the car roof. Construction of the new Central Line trains started in the late-summer of 1990 and the first 4-car train to be delivered arrived at Ruislip depot on 17 May 1992. A 3-car unit of 1962 Stock (1422-9423-1423) was fitted with redundant compressors from the 1986 Stock and was used as a pilot unit for transferring newly delivered units of 1992 Stock between Ruislip and Northfields for trials on the South Ealing test tracks.

The first train entered passenger service on the Central Line on 7 April 1993. This introduced one-person operation and Correct Side Door Enable (CSDE) on the Central Line for the first time. With only two trains outstanding to be delivered, enough were available for the full Monday to Friday service to be worked with new trains from Monday 20 February 1995.

Since new, a number of visible and audible changes and modifications have been made to the 1992 Stock fleet. First was the fitting of tripcock/ATP reset bars beneath the driver's window, enabling resetting to be done without the train operator having to get down onto the track. The first stage of Automatic Train Protection commenced on the western branches to North Acton on 19 June 1995, where trains changed between ATP and tripcock modes. By 10 November 1997 the whole of the Central Line had been converted to ATP. Trainstops were no longer required and subsequently removed. On the 1992 Tube Stock the reset bars were soon removed, although some DM cars still have a small part of the fixing in place.

4-car trains of 1992 Tube Stock operate the short Waterloo & City Line and remain in their distinctive Network SouthEast livery. A 4-car train has just arrived at Bank. The destination in fact comprises a yellow-on-black sticker.
Brian Hardy

The unreliability of the illuminated train set number and destination display equipment led to their replacement by early-1996 and by mid-1996 respectively. In the case of the latter, it was necessary to carry card destination indicators in the front cab door for a year or so. The audible 'door open' bleeps gave way to a single bleep by early-1996. This modification also incorporated the retiming of the voice announcement to be more accurate at station stops. The armrests between the seats have not stood the test of time, the antisocial element of society soon discovering how weak the fittings were. Those that were not broken or destroyed were removed. A more durable and heavy-duty type of armrest was tried on seven units (91011, 91021, 91073, 91087, 91135, 91287 and 91337) from mid-1996 but these, too, were subsequently removed and it appears that that the trains will be without armrests for the foreseeable future.

The replacement rolling stock for the Waterloo & City Line comprised ten 2-car units of 1992 Tube Stock, which were an 'add-on' order to London Underground's eighty-five 8-car trains. A total of 20 cars were required, with 4-car trains being required for service. Each 2-car unit is formed of an 'E' DM and an 'F' NDM, although they are, in most respects, identical to the A-B two-car units on the Central Line. Being then owned by Network SouthEast, the only main visible difference was that the trains were finished in a variation of the NSE livery – predominantly blue and white with a thin red line at floor level. All ten E-F units were delivered to LUL's Ruislip depot in three consignments in March 1993, where they were commissioned for test running prior to being transferred to the Waterloo & City Line. Whilst under test, the trains in their distinctive livery visited most parts of the Central Line, albeit without passengers. These trips were always in 8-car formations, the only time that the DM couplers would actually be used under normal service conditions, as on the Waterloo & City, 4-car trains are the norm. The interiors are also the same as on the Central Line trains, the only difference being in the style of safety notices and, whilst in Network SouthEast ownership, the lack of route maps. British Rail identified the stock as Class 482 and unit numbers were from 501–510. DM 'E' cars are numbered 65501–65510 and NDM 'F' cars 67501–67510. Each are formed into easily identifiable units, 65501-67501 being unit 482.501 and so on up to 65510-67510 (482.510).

Trains were transferred from Ruislip to Waterloo by road over three weekends in May and June 1993. The first test run from Waterloo to Bank took place on 27 June and driver training commenced the following day. Timetabled 'ghost' running started on 12 July and passengers were carried on the modernised Waterloo & City Line from Monday 19 July 1993, all units being in service at some time during that day.

On 1 April 1994 the operation of the Waterloo & City Line was taken over by London Underground. Being the Easter weekend, the line was closed for staff training and familiarisation, reopening under its new owners on Tuesday 5 April. The line was organised as part of the Central Line Business Unit, which provided the operational and maintenance staff. More recently, management of the line has passed to the Bakerloo Line, although staff (from Leytonstone and Hainault respectively) continue to be provided by the Central Line.

On transfer of control to LUL, the former NSE 'class', 'flash' and 'unit' numbers were removed, although they remain on the inner end NDM 'F' cars. Like their counterparts on the Central Line, these trains, too, suffered with set number and destination display problems and from October 1995 until February 1996, card train-set numbers were carried in the front cab door. To provide spares for the Central Line fleet, vinyl destination stickers replaced the electronic equipment in May 2000, while at the same time, inter-car barrier fixings were fitted. From 8 July 1996, 'Correct Side Door Enable' equipment was commissioned on the line. This equipment, also operational on the Central Line (along with all other lines apart from the Victoria Line), is designed to prevent train operators opening passenger doors on the wrong side of the trains at stations.

Interior of a 1992 Stock train on the Waterloo & City Line, whose clientele have seen the armrests inside the cars remain in place. Capital Transport

1995 and 1996 TUBE STOCK

In April 2002,
1996 Tube Stock
DM 96002 is at the rear of
a train seen entering
Stratford station, the
eastern extremity of the
Jubilee Line Extension,
which was opened in
1999. DM 96002 was
exhibited at the
Birmingham Railtech
exhibition and at
Canary Wharf at the
end of May 1996,
before being delivered to
LUL in August 1996.
Brian Hardy

The 1995 and 1996 Tube Stocks are almost identical to each other in appearance but there are equipment differences between each type. All trains were assembled by GEC Alsthom Metro-Cammell Ltd (now Alstom) at Washwood Heath, Birmingham. However, the car body shells were built in Barcelona in Spain, the train doors in Canada and the bogies by ACR at Le Creusot in France.

A main difference between this and the previous build of stock (the 1992 Stock for the Central Line) comes from its origins for the Jubilee Line trains. A once proposed scheme was for them to be a mix of 1983 Stock, refurbished and converted to run with newly-built cars to make up the 59 trains required. To enable all the cars to have a similar look, the saloon windows on the new cars would have to match those on the older cars, and would thus not curve up into the roof. For this reason, both the 1995 and 1996 stocks have standard height saloon windows.

First to be delivered were examples of 1996 Tube Stock which will thus be considered first. The fifty-nine 6-car trains of 1996 Tube Stock were built exclusively for the Jubilee Line, which was extended from Green Park to Stratford via Waterloo, London Bridge, Canary Wharf and North Greenwich. Between Canning Town and Stratford, it parallels the National Rail Silverlink Metro service, which runs between North Woolwich and Richmond. The new extension opened in stages in 1999, but many of the new trains of 1996 Tube Stock had previously entered service on the original Jubilee Line between Stanmore and Charing Cross, replacing the 1983 Tube Stock. A new major maintenance depot with extensive open-air stabling sidings was built at Stratford, although trains continue to stable in Neasden depot and Stanmore sidings.

DM 96060 of 1996 Tube Stock is seen at the rear of a train at Bond Street on 27 April 2002, on the occasion of a disrupted service – normally train set numbers on the Jubilee Line are in the 3xx series, this being in the 7xx series and on a short working to North Greenwich.
Capital Transport

The public had an early glimpse of the new 1996 Tube Stock when DM 96002 was exhibited at the Railtech exhibition at the NEC in Birmingham, which was followed by a three-day display at Canary Wharf on 29–31 May 1996.

The first train of 1996 Tube Stock was delivered to Ruislip depot on 18 July 1996, and the following month went to Northfields for trials on the South Ealing test tracks. Three 4-car units of 1962 Tube Stock were specially converted for use as 'pilots', the first being painted in an olive green livery. The other two units remained in unpainted aluminium. On each transfer of stock, one 4-car pilot unit took one 3-car unit of new stock – the new trains were unable to operate on their own as they would interfere with signalling equipment.

The pre-passenger service history of the 1996 Tube Stock is complex, which was due, in part, to the late completion of the Jubilee Line Extension. The first train to arrive at Stratford Market depot comprised units 96003+96004 in December 1996. Because the depot was not at that stage connected to the main Underground network (at Green Park Junction), transfer was by road from Ruislip depot. From April to November 1997 eleven other units arrived at Stratford in the same way, the first by rail via the connection at Green Park being on 26 March 1998. The first train to run on the Jubilee Line tracks was 96003+96004 on 6 January 1997. This was followed by a press launch at West Ham three days later. On 13 August 1997 another 'special' train (units 96024+96023) operated for school children between Stratford and Canning Town, hauled by Schoma diesels. This was also the first train to run under its own power to North Greenwich and is recorded as doing so on 1 September 1997. On the existing Jubilee Line, a press launch took place using units 96012+96011 on 14 February 1997, but it was to be just over another ten months before the new trains entered service on the existing line.

That took place almost without ceremony with one round trip between Wembley Park and Charing Cross in the afternoon of 24 December 1997 with units 96030+96025. Normal entry into passenger service coincided with (another) press launch on 6 January 1998, this date often (incorrectly) being quoted as the first day in passenger service of the 1996 Tube Stock.

Meanwhile, delays with the new extension and difficulties with the new trains continued. Because they were being delivered at a rate faster than they could be commissioned, and with no new 'extension' to run them on (the Jubilee Line Extension was intended to be up and running in early-1998), 18½ 6-car trains were put into store at various locations. Four were stored at Cockfosters, 3½ at Upminster, while seven went off LUL metals completely to the MOD complex at Kineton in Warwickshire. Two trains were also stored in the permanent way sidings at the back of Neasden depot and two more in Charing Cross sidings, albeit briefly. In addition, six of the earlier-delivered trains returned to Birmingham for modifications before entering passenger service. Furthermore, the later than anticipated delivery of the Northern Line's 1995 Tube Stock saw two trains of 1996 Stock transferred to Edgware for crew familiarisation. Units 96006+96005 were transferred in April 1998, being replaced by 96022+96021 in July, the former being required for modifications back in Birmingham. The latter returned to Ruislip in March 1998.

The exterior of the Northern Line's 1995 Tube Stock is very similar to that on the Jubilee Line, save for having conventional front cab 'M' doors. DM 51655 leads a southbound train into Brent Cross on 13 June 1999. The space between the end of the platform and the northbound starting signal on the left used to be the platform extension for 9-car trains that ran on the Northern Line between 1937 and 1939. Kim Rennie

Left The inside of a 1996 Stock car, showing the space provided for wheelchairs around the door area in the centre section of each car. Capital Transport

Right This full size mock up of a 1996 Stock cab end is now at London's Transport Museum's depot at Acton. Capital Transport

Left The Northern Line chose to have pairs of tip-up seats around the centre door sections, rather than perches. It should be noted that in this area, the passenger emergency alarm handles are at a lower position than in the rest of the train. Capital Transport

The Jubilee Line Extension opened in a number of stages, the first between Stratford and North Greenwich on 14 May 1999, followed by North Greenwich to Bermondsey on 17 September 1999 and then Waterloo one week later. The link was completed on 20 November 1999 when trains ran through between the 'old' and 'new' sections. Not all units had entered service at this time, however, and it was not until 31 July 2001 that the last (96104) entered passenger service.

The trains of 1996 Tube Stock are formed into 3-car M-T-UNDM units, using the standard 'A' end (even numbers) and 'D' end (odd numbers) system of identification. They are finished in London Underground's Corporate livery. Like the 1992 Tube Stock on the Central Line, the cars are built to the standard tube profile by welding full-length longitudinal aluminium extrusions and thus the sliding doors are on the exterior of the car body. The front cab door incorporates pull-down detrainment steps, should it be necessary to detrain passengers onto the track. The door will also slide back should it be necessary for passengers to pass through from one train to another. Illumination for this is provided by two lights in the head/tail light group below the driving cab windows. The LCD destination indicator and train set number are located above the front cab door. The order included 20 de-icing trailers on 'A'-end units.

Inside, all seats are longitudinal, there being seats for 32 passengers in DM cars and 34 each in trailer and UNDM cars. Around the door areas in the centre saloon section, moquette-covered perches are provided, along with those at the car ends on either side of the communicating door. The resultant larger interior spaces around the double-doorway areas makes it possible to accommodate wheelchairs. For the visually impaired, bright yellow grab rails and poles have been used throughout. The interior colour scheme is a pleasing finish of cream with bright blue uprights around the doorway areas and purple armrests. In addition to the now standard public address equipment, automatic passenger announcements can be made, either automatically or initiated by the train operator. The operation of the emergency pull-down alarm handles for passengers provides a talk-back facility with the train operator. Some of the emergency handles are located at a lower position for use by disabled passengers.

Between cars, rubber inter-car gap protectors have also been provided at the car ends, to prevent passengers falling between cars. This and the 1995 Stock was the first to have them from new. All other stocks have since been fitted with inter-car 'barriers', comprising a plastic 'curtain' hooked to the corner of each car.

In the train operator's cab, a combined traction/brake controller with 'deadman' device is incorporated within the arm of the train operator's adjustable seat as on 1992 Tube Stock. CCTV is provided for observing station platforms and a display for the train operator of the Train Management System is provided on a screen on the right-hand side of the cab. Trains are currently worked in conventional OPO mode – automatic train operation may become a reality at some time in the future.

The 1996 Stock is powered by four frame-mounted 3-phase induction motors per motor car. All four motors are fed from a single voltage-sourced inverter, derived from one of those used on main line Class 465 Networker trains. The system is capable of regenerative braking and carries a fully rated dynamic brake resistor and thus regenerative, rheostatic and friction braking are all available. Electrical loads on the trains are fed at either 630V d.c. in the case of traction drives and saloon heating, 240V a.c. for saloon ventilation and 52V d.c. for the train's control functions and all other loads. The bogies are conventional 2-axle, fabricated H-frames, fitted with rubber suspension.

To allow for passenger traffic on the Jubilee Line exceeding planned estimates, provision was made for an additional trailer to be inserted in each 'D' end unit, between the UNDM and existing trailer. If built, these cars would be numbered 96601–96717, odd numbers only. It now seems likely that not only will the additional trailers be built under the Public Private Partnership contracts for the London Underground, but the Jubilee Line fleet may be increased by a further 12 trains.

The 1995 Tube Stock was also built by GEC Alsthom Metro-Cammell Ltd, (now Alstom) under a private finance initiative, and has been be leased to London Underground for 25 years to provide the service on the Northern Line. Like their 1996 Stock counterparts, their history before entering service has been lengthy and varied, to say the least. One DM car (51502) of the new trains was displayed in the Lord Mayor's Show in London on 9 November 1996.

The first train of 1995 Tube Stock was delivered to Ruislip depot on 20 December 1996 but it was to be another four months before the second train arrived. Testing on the South Ealing test tracks with unit 51701 began in early 1997, while its other half (unit 51501) was the first to arrive at Golders Green on 24 April 1997. These trains, too, suffered with commissioning difficulties and a number had to be stored before entering service. Because there was no spare storage space on the Underground, between June and October 1998 twenty-six 6-car trains were sent to MOD Kineton for storage and a further eight were delivered new to Kineton direct from Birmingham. These eight trains arrived at Ruislip during the autumn of 1999. Of the other 26, a total of 12 had first to return to Birmingham before returning to London Underground. The first three trains of 1995 Tube Stock were delivered with front cab doors as employed on the Jubilee Line's 1996 Tube Stock. However, it was the desire to have 'conventional' cab doors on the Northern Line and these three trains were later modified to Northern Line 'standard', being returned to Birmingham before entering service.

The 1995 and 1996 Tube Stocks for the Northern and Jubilee lines respectively were fitted with inter-car barriers from new, comprising solid rubber uprights at the car ends, an example being seen at Edgware on the Northern Line.
Capital Transport

Entry into passenger service began on 12 June 1998 (units 51514+51513) and gradually began to replace the 1956/59/62 Tube Stock on the Northern Line. The new trains operated in OPO mode from the beginning and guards were replaced in a carefully planned programme. The last train of 1959 Tube Stock ran on the Northern Line on 27 January 2000, and so ended guards on the London Underground. By that time 97 out of the 106 new trains had been commissioned for service, which was sufficient for providing the 84-train peak-hour service. The other nine trains then entered passenger service, the last (51598+51599) on 10 April 2001.

Whilst the three-car units (M-T-UNDM) are nominally regarded as 'A' or 'D' end units and are numbered appropriately, all units are completely reversible so that a train may comprise two units of one type. This has been necessary because the Kennington loop on the Northern Line results in trains becoming 'turned' during the course of their duty and reversible units provide maximum rolling stock flexibility in train make-up.

The trains are currently being driven under manual conditions by a train operator but have the facility to permit ATP and ATO to be equipped at a later date. Whilst the Jubilee and Northern Line trains are quite similar in appearance, those for the Northern Line incorporate pairs of tip-up seats by the door stand-backs in the centre section of the saloon, a yellow/black/grey seating moquette and black armrests. Trains are equipped with in-car video recording equipment. Rubber inter-car gap protectors have also been provided at the car ends, to prevent passengers falling between cars. Unlike other tube stock built in the 1990s, whose five-digit numbers all begin with '9', the 1995 Tube Stock breaks tradition by beginning with '5'. In the order of 106 6-car trains, there are 26 de-icing trailers, equally split between 'A' and 'D' units.

The controls, indications and platform CCTV monitors are situated directly in the train operator's line of sight, while the a.c. traction package uses IGBT technology instead of gate-turn-off thyristors, as on the Jubilee Line trains.

SURFACE STOCK

A60/62 STOCK

From the timetable introduced in May 2001, in off-peak periods Amersham trains make an additional stop at Wembley Park in both directions. One such service is seen arriving at Wembley Park on 27 May 2002. Brian Hardy

The origins of what became the A Stock can be traced back prior to the Second World War, for the electrification of the Metropolitan Line to Amersham and Chesham was proposed under the 1935–40 New Works Programme. Mock-ups of differing designs were built at Acton Works but it was not until 1946 that two experimental trailers were built on withdrawn T Stock underframes. Not only were different interiors trialled but the two cars had air-operated sliding doors, for which an additional guard was carried on the train. Once the trials had been concluded, the two cars were scrapped.

The electrification of the Metropolitan Line from Rickmansworth to Amersham and Chesham and the provision of two additional tracks from Harrow-on-the-Hill to north of Moor Park (Watford South Junction, where the Watford line diverges) did not in the event restart until 1959. A total of 31 new trains, to be known as A60 Stock, were ordered from Cravens Ltd of Sheffield. The stock comprised 124 driving motor cars and 124 trailers, being formed into four car units (M-T-T-M). Numbering was 5000–5123 (DMs) and 6000–6123 (trailers). The first train of A60 Stock entered passenger service on 12 June 1961 (units 5004 and 5008). A further order for 27 trains of A Stock, almost identical to the first batch, was provided to replace the F and P stocks on the Uxbridge line. This second batch was designated A62 Stock and comprised 108 driving motor cars (5124–5231) and 108 trailers (6124–6231). The A62 Stock followed on without

4-car double-ended units operate on the East London Line, the trains in service at peak times now being six instead of five, which had been the maximum until 1998. DM 5234 is at the north end of a train at New Cross Gate and comprises four cars that had lain derelict since 1981. They were repaired and returned to service in 1994, forming part of the first refurbished train of A Stock. Alan Kybird

interruption after the A60 batch and all A Stock trains were in service by December 1963. All driving motor cars were provided with fully automatic couplers, similar to those introduced on the 1960 Tube Stock, enabling any driving motor car to be coupled to another. (The versatility of the A Stock fleet was demonstrated in 1981, when two 'D' end DMs were formed in one unit – 'D' end DM 5043 temporarily replaced 'A' DM 5056, the latter being under repair).

Interior seating was arranged transversely with an off-centre gangway, allowing seats to be arranged in pairs on one side and in groups of three on the other. The DM cars seated 54 passengers and had in addition, four tip-up seats at the end furthest from the cab, while trailers seated 58 passengers. Small luggage racks were provided above window level.

A60 and A62 Stock units were interchangeable until converted for one-person operation (OPO), and operated in 8-car formations of two 4-car units. The practice of operating single 4-car units in off-peak times was discontinued in 1981. However, the Chalfont – Chesham shuttle service continues to be operated by a single unit and 4-car trains have operated on the East London Line from June 1977 until the end of April 1985 and from May 1987 until 24 March 1995, when the line closed for repair and refurbishment. A Stock returned to the East London Line when it reopened on 25 March 1998.

Compared to some other stocks, changes to unit formations have been few, but following a collision at Kilburn in December 1984, four cars salvaged from it (5028-6028-6117-5117) were formed into one unit in June 1985 and renumbered 5232-6232-6233-5233 in August 1985. DM 5008 replaced 5034 in July 1985 each being renumbered with the (new) 5008 (ex-5034) and 5009 being stored damaged, along with trailers 6008 and 6009.

In the meantime, plans were drawn up to convert and adapt the A60/62 Stock for one-person operation. This would involve extensive alterations, but would be more financially viable than ordering new stock and scrapping trains that still had some 15–20 years operational life left in them. A total of fifty-six of the original fifty-eight 8-car trains remained and were thus converted to OPO between April 1985 and September 1986, some at Ruislip depot, but mostly at Acton Works. It was this conversion that reduced the flexibility of the stock, as the fleet was then divided into 44 'A' end units, 44 'D' end units and 24 double-ended units. A total of 88 DMs were thus relegated to the middle of train formations and the expense of high-intensity headlights, door controls and missile-proof windscreens on those cars was then avoided. From OPO conversion, coupling was strictly 'A' to 'D', with the relevant end letters being applied to all DM ends. These were colour-coded red and green, and only green 'A' and 'D' ends could be coupled together for service. The first converted train in crew-operated mode was in service from 19 November 1985 (units 5038 and 5227), while OPO on the Metropolitan Line commenced on 29 September 1986.

Not included in the OPO conversion programme were stored cars 5008 (ex-5034), 5009, 6008, 6009, 6029, 6116 and 6171, along with unit 5036-6036-6037-5037 which had been cannibalised for spares and had not run in service since July 1977. In addition, cars 5170, 6170, 5029, 5116 and 5171 were scrapped between 1981 and 1987.

Interior of an A Stock, showing the windows cut into the car ends on refurbishment. Although the interior comprises new materials and fittings, the trains retain their 3+2 seating configuration. Brian Hardy

An A Stock car that has not carried passengers since 1977 is trailer 6036, which now operates each autumn as a Rail Treatment Car in a double-ended unit, making five cars in all. It has been modified to work with refurbished stock and is seen sporting the Corporate livery at Amersham on 26 November 2000.
Paul Bradley

In 1986 trailer 6036 was converted at Acton Works into a 'Rail Treatment Car', to dispense Sandite (an adhesion improver) on running rails. This is particularly necessary north of Rickmansworth on the Metropolitan Line each autumn in the leaf-fall season. The converted car was formed into a 4-car double-ended unit of A Stock (making five cars in all) and underwent tests in the autumn of 1986. Tests were successful and during each autumn from 1987 onwards the car has been inserted into a double-ended unit. During the period of non-use after the 1986 experiments, the body of car 6036 was repainted off white and its roof in Metropolitan Line maroon, and trial blue lettering/car numbers were applied, prior to adopting a policy for future A Stock overhauls at Neasden, which started in mid-1987. When the refurbishment of the A Stock eventually started, trailer 6036 was repainted in corporate colours in 1996 to match the stock it would be working with during the autumn months.

The seven units that work the East London Line were the first members of A Stock in passenger service to be exterior painted. Unit 5066 was completed first at Ruislip in November 1988 in off-white with blue doors, grey roofs and red cab ends. The other six units followed in 1989–90, but these were painted by Vic Berry of Leicester where they were taken by road from and to Ruislip (initially) and (later) Neasden. Units 5058, 5062, 5064 and 5232 were painted similarly to 5066 (with minor differences), while unit 5056 was painted in off-white below waist level and blue above waist level, but still with red cab ends and grey roof. The last unit to be painted (5122) was in 'red doors' livery – off-white with blue 'skirt', red doors and cab ends but with a white roof. This was the livery that was chosen on painting schemes for all passenger stock, except that the roof colour became grey. As the A Stock for the East London Line is maintained at Neasden, it was not uncommon for these painted units to work on the Metropolitan Line to Uxbridge, Watford and Amersham, which indeed happened on a daily basis after the East London Line closed for modernisation in March 1995 and until the units went for refurbishment.

In preparation for the intended refurbishment of A Stock, two cars (5132 and 6132) were selected for trials. The work was done by Metro-Cammell in 1989 and the exteriors were painted in the same style as unit 5056. Inside trailer 6132, panelling and seating moquette was replaced and new flooring fitted. More substantial changes were made to the inside of 5132 and both cars were given pull-down hopper windows. It was decided, however, that further trials were required and the complete 4-car unit (5132-6132-6133-5133) returned to Metro-Cammell in February 1990. The 4-car unit was delivered back to Neasden in early June 1990 and the exterior was painted into 'red doors' livery with grey roof. Inside, the colour scheme was cream and pale pink with a dark grey area around ankle level. Floor-to-ceiling poles were fitted and these along with other grab poles, were finished in a pale blue. The old draught screens to the ceilings were replaced by those finishing at head height only. New vandal-resistant car seats were individually shaped and a new moquette was used. All four cars were given hopper windows in place of the former tilting quarter lights. The unit re-entered service on 8 August 1990.

To provide additional stock to cover for the A Stock refurbishment programme, eight of the damaged and almost 'derelict' A60 Stock cars (5008-6008-6009-5009 and 5036-6116-6037-5037) were repaired and reinstated to operational condition, forming two double-ended 4-car units. To that end they were taken to BREL Derby by road in August 1990. Lack of funding initially prevented the refurbishment programme going ahead in 1991 and the repair of the eight derelict cars took longer than anticipated. However, cars 5036, 5037, 6037 and 6116 returned to Neasden in August 1992 in unrefurbished condition. By this time, the go-ahead had been given to refurbish the A Stock and the interior fittings for 5036-6116-6037-5037 were obtained from unit 5173 which had been transferred to ABB in August 1992 to be part of the first refurbished 8-car train (along with 5008-6008-6009-5009). Cars 5036, 6037 and 5037 were renumbered (respectively) 5116, 6117 and 5117 in April 1993 and the complete 4-car unit (5116-6116-6117-5117) re-entered service on 7th May 1993.

Two other instances of A Stock renumbering have also taken place. Since 1986, DM 5209 has taken the place of collision-damaged 5121 and in March 1993 DM 5209 was renumbered 5121 after being converted into a double-ended DM. The other three cars of the unit (5208-6208-6209) had been stored since OPO conversion in 1986 and in August 1992 DM 5208 replaced 5218 and was accordingly renumbered. The original 5218 was the one which has been involved with suspension trials for many years and was fitted for a time with air metacone suspension and D Stock bogies. This, along with the original damaged 5121, and with trailers 6208 and 6209 and 6029 and 6171, made a total of six cars which were scrapped in 1994.

The total stock for the Metropolitan Line (and East London Line) now comprises 44 'A' end units, 43 'D' end units and 26 double-ended units, making 56½ 8-car trains.

The refurbishment of A Stock eventually commenced in 1992, the first train comprising ex-derelict unit 5008-6008-6009-5009 which became double-ended de-icing unit 5234-6234-6235-5235, along

A62 DM 5173 is seen at Amersham at the rear of a train from Baker Street. This DM is unique in that the roof dome has a slightly different profile.
Brian Hardy

with 5172-6172-6173-5173. The complete train returned to Neasden on 23 April 1994, entering service on the Metropolitan Line on 22 September 1994. DM 5173, however, remains unique, in that its roof dome has a slightly different profile. This was because there was no spare DM dome then available and a dome from a trailer car had to be used and adapted instead. Two single 'A'-end units (5000 and 5004) have been fitted with de-icing equipment on refurbishment. Refurbished trains are fitted with Correct Side Door Enable equipment, which was introduced on the Metropolitan Line on 25 November 1996. The ventilator over the destination blind has been removed and the whistle re-positioned in the dome of the grey roof. Inside, the traditional maple wood flooring has been replaced by rubber matting and a new ceiling design incorporates new lighting. The gravity tilting opening quarter lights have been replaced by spring hopper windows. Windows have been fitted at the trailing ends of DM cars and both ends of trailers for added passenger security. The Metropolitan Line coloured grab poles have replaced and supplemented the former grab handles and interior panelling is off-white with a pale pink around the window areas.

The programme was completed in early-1998 with unit 5024 re-entering service on 11 February 1998.

The A Stock, now over 40 years old, is to be replaced under the PPP proposals for the London Underground. This is unlikely to be before 2010, however, by which time the fleet, still almost intact, will be approaching 50 years old, earning a unique place in London Underground history. There have been, of course, a few examples of maybe half a dozen reaching or getting very close to 50 years but these have always been the last few of a much larger fleet that has been cannibalised to keep the last few alive. The fact that much of the A Stock may survive to its 50th birthday must be a real triumph for the designers.

C Stock provides all of the service on the Circle and Hammersmith & City lines. A Circle Line train is seen at King's Cross St Pancras.
Capital Transport

The Circle and Hammersmith & City lines were operated by 6-car trains of converted CO and CP Stock of 1937–39 vintage, until the delivery of the C69 Stock enabled the CO/CP Stock to be transferred to the District Line to replace the last of the Q Stock. The letter 'C' indicates 'Circle' – there has been no B Stock in modern times. The first train of C69 Stock entered service on 28 September 1970 (units 5522, 5523 and 5524) and all were in service by December 1971.

The new stock comprised 106 driving motor cars (5501–5606) and 106 trailers (6501–6606), formed into 2-car semi-permanently coupled units (M-T). This equated to thirty-five 6-car trains, plus a spare 2-car unit. All units were identical and at the outer ends of each a fully-automatic reversible coupler was fitted. The six-cars for each train could therefore be formed M-T+T-M+T-M or M-T+M-T+T-M.

Each car has four sets of double passenger doors on each side, with seating capacity reduced in consequence to 32. On the lines which the stock operates, the majority of passenger journeys are of short distances and so the additional doors were introduced to allow increased speed in boarding and alighting in busy periods. Each pair of doors is separated by double-glazed car windows. On the driving motor cars the cab door is also air operated, being independently controlled. The door control panels were located in the cab, as on the O Stock previously working on the Hammersmith & City Line. Public address is fitted to enable the driver to make announcements to passengers. A 'selective close' facility is provided at terminal stations in cold weather.

When new, 14 trailers (6543–6556) were fitted with de-icing equipment, but three of these (6554–6556) were decommissioned prior to refurbishment. Air metacone suspension was provided on the trains from new, following trials on A62 Stock DM car 5218. Rheostatic braking as on 1967 stock was also fitted. Provision was also made in the design for the trains to be converted to One Person Operation and all cars were modified in 1983–84. Ceiling-mounted fans were located at each door position for heating, being thermostatically controlled. A hydraulic parking brake was fitted in each DM cab, and all cars had illuminated interior advertisement panels on the bulkhead dividing the saloon from the doorway area.

To replace the 6-car trains of CO/CP Stock operating the Wimbledon to Edgware Road section of the District Line, eleven 6-car

trains of C77 Stock were ordered from Metro-Cammell. Delivery commenced in July 1977. The cars are similar to the C69 Stock and likewise are formed into 2-car reversible units (M-T) with an automatic coupler at each outer end. In consequence, the maintenance of C77 Stock trains is carried out at Hammersmith depot. The first train of C77 Stock entered service on the Hammersmith & City Line on 12 December 1977 (units 5701, 5702 and 5703).

The C77 Stock order in fact comprised one additional DM car. This was numbered 5585 and replaced the original C69 DM which was bomb-damaged beyond repair at West Ham in March 1976. Its trailer, 6585, was less severely damaged and was repaired at Acton Works. Interior car heaters on C77 Stock initially comprised panels below the draught screen at floor level but during 1979/80 additional heaters were fitted up to draughtscreen level, covered with a blue aerowalk material.

The intention to operate the C Stock as One-Person-Operated trains was frustrated by protracted negotiations between management and unions and it was not until 26 March 1984 that OPO was introduced on the Hammersmith & City Line. The Circle Line followed suit from 22 October 1984 and the Wimbledon – Edgware Road section of the District Line (along with the District main line) from 4 November 1985.

The C Stock then entered a period of relative stability until consideration was given to refurbishing it. C77/69 Stock unit 5585-6585 was chosen as the prototype and work was undertaken at BREL, Derby in 1989. The exterior of both cars was painted blue above waist level and white beneath, with a red driving cab front and grey roof. Both cars had the maple wood flooring replaced by light grey grooved moulded flooring and the trailing ends were fitted with windows to improve visibility between cars, thus enhancing passenger security. Other changes included the fitting of a spring-applied parking brake. Inside DM 5585 new seating moquette and suspended rectangular yellow grab rails for standing passengers were fitted. More substantial changes were made to trailer 6585, where the transverse seats were replaced by longitudinal seating with the loss of six seat positions. The fitting of a shunting control cabinet to the uncoupling end of 6585 caused the loss of one further seat and thus the number of seats in this car was reduced from 32 to

Interior of a C Stock train, showing the end windows that were added on refurbishment, along with the green, mauve and yellow squares as the seat décor. Much use has been made of Circle Line yellow on the grab rails.
Capital Transport

25, although standing capacity was greatly increased. The ceiling bulkheads in 6585 were redesigned, eliminating the illuminated advertisement positions, while the draught screens were reduced in size – the grab poles and glass slanted inwards towards the body above waist level.

Having been displayed to the public, the unit entered service on 22 November 1989. The success of the refurbishment led to a contract being awarded to RFS Industries of Doncaster for the C69 and C77 Stock fleet to be refurbished and painted, the first units being transferred to RFS in 1990. The external finish is in the LUL 'red doors' corporate livery and the internal finish is from a design by Cre'active. The interiors of all cars retained their 32 seat capacity, but all seats were longitudinal and in pairs, each pair separated by armrests. This seating arrangement allows a greater area for standing passengers and makes it even harder (if not impossible) for the undesirables to put their feet on the opposite seats – nevertheless, those of a slovenly disposition still put their feet on the grab poles! Additionally, twin yellow grab rails run the length of the car at head height in place of strap hangers. Along the roof line, slots have been cut into the car roof to expel air, should fans be fitted at a later date (trailer 6513 was fitted with air cooling equipment in refurbished condition but this has now been removed). The refurbishment also included replacing the air suspension using rubber 'blobs' (as on D Stock), the provision of new bogies and spring-applied parking brakes. Trailer 6527, which had grilles in the ventilation slots above the car windows, was converted to standard. Trailer 6567, however, retains its tinted glass car windows, a legacy of interior cooling trials in the mid-1970s.

The last C Stock to be refurbished returned to LUL on 9 April 1994, re-entering service on 5 May 1994. On a refurbished C69 or C77 Stock train, it is no longer possible to distinguish between the two types in appearance.

One unit of C69 Stock was not included for refurbishment, being 5606-6606 which had been fitted with experimental traction equipment by Kiepe in 1974. The equipment was in need of replacement and required extensive modification to convert it back to standard. It was declared withdrawn, having been taken out of service in January 1991. In May 1993 it was taken to RFS Doncaster, ultimately for disposal.

A second all-over-advert train was launched on 12 February 1998, comprising C69 units 5573+5555+5593 advertising 'Yellow Pages'. This was painted yellow with coloured stick-on advertising features. The seating also had special 'Yellow Pages' moquette. The advertising vinyls were removed in May 1999, but it was not until August 1999 that the train was transferred to Acton Works for repainting back to Corporate livery, which was completed in November 1999. Since then, there have been no other all-over-advert schemes on London's Underground rolling stock.

Since the previous edition of this book, the C Stock fleet has undergone several programmes of engineering modifications, most of them being related to train equipment. However, some will be noticed by the passenger and these are summarised as follows.

From the autumn of 1997 trains were fitted with Digitised Voice Announcers (DVA), which are programmed by the train operator. From the same time, shatter-proof cab windows replaced the originals – these have a black surround to them, which changed their front end appearance considerably. Although the C Stock had inter-car barriers fitted between the trailing ends of cars, it was not until 2000–2001 that they were fitted to the cab ends of driving motor cars (because DM cars work in the middle of train formations) giving them a 'blinkered' appearance. From late-2001 car numbers on DM cars were additionally applied in blue on the grey roof dome, to the left of the destination blind box, while from the same time, another series of modifications began and saw the original refurbished seating moquette (small squares of mauve, yellow and green on grey or black) replaced. The new design (known as 'spatter' moquette because it gives the impression of paint being 'spattered') incorporates the same colour scheme, but the seats themselves are much deeper and far more comfortable.

After some ten or more years in service, the refurbished C Stock began to look a little tired and a programme of improvements was begun in 2001. Of cosmetic note to the passenger is that the grab rails have been repainted, but probably more importantly, deeper and more comfortable seats have been fitted. The same colour scheme has been used on the moquette but is arranged as if 'paint-spattered'.
Capital Transport

D Stock departing Turnham Green in August 2001. By May 2002 most D Stock trains had blue numbers applied on the DM ends, with large blue numbers on the sides at cantrail level. Brian Hardy

The D Stock comprises 75 trains which replaced the bulk of the District Line's CO/CP and R stocks between 1980 and 1983. Each train is composed of six cars, but each car is about 60ft long and a train of D Stock is approximately the same length as the 7-car train it replaced. The train formation is as used for the 1973 Tube Stock on the Piccadilly Line. Most trains have two single-cab units with automatic couplers on the middle UNDM cars, and 65 east and 65 west facing single cab units were built. Twenty double-cab units with automatic couplers at each driving end were also built and these units were the first type to be delivered. D Stock is numbered 7000–7129 (DMs), 7500–7539 (DMs with automatic couplers), 8000–8129 (UNDMs), 17000–17129 (trailers) and even numbers only from 17500–17538 (trailers used in double-cab units). Trailers 17035 and 17077 exchanged numbers in 1994 when they were out of service with long-term defects.

Each of the four passenger doorways on each side of the car is 3ft 6ins wide, 1ft less than each double doorway on CO/CP and R stocks. A single leaf sliding door is fitted at each opening. Draught screens are set back from the door openings by about 8ins. DM cars seat 44, trailers and UNDMs seat 48. One transverse seat bay on each side of the car is provided in the centre section of all cars – all other seats are longitudinal. A new seating moquette was introduced which was a mix of yellow, orange and brown. This was also employed on the 1983 Tube Stock and on many London buses in the same era.

A modified form of passenger door control (PDC) was incorporated with illuminating 'Press to Open' buttons for passenger use. Each doorway has three 'passenger open' buttons, two inside and one outside. The 'selective close' facility for passenger comfort is provided as on C69/77 Stock and a new 'selective reopen' facility was installed whereby it is possible to reopen only the doors on those cars where they have failed to close properly. The door controls are located in the driving cabs.

To improve riding quality, a new type of bogie was tested on A62 Stock DM car 5218 for use on D Stock. This incorporates suspension using two hemispherical rubber cushions supporting a coil spring and replaces an earlier plan to use air bags. Fans are installed in the car ceilings for ventilation and 'Pyro-bar' type car heaters are also installed.

A new type of driver's control handle was incorporated and operates in the 'fore' and 'aft' positions. This type of controller was tried out on the experimental 1935 Tube Stock, but the handle has to be kept twisted while the train is in motion (this position being equivalent to the dead man's handle) and moved forward for motoring and back for braking. The driver's seat is a swivelling design instead of a 'pull down' and adjusts up and down as well as forwards and backwards. As on the 1973 Tube Stock, a fault-finding Train Equipment Panel (TEP) was provided (with modifications) as were air-operating sliding cab doors. A spring-applied parking brake is fitted instead of the hydraulic type fitted to previous stocks. Only one compressor is fitted on each single-cab unit, but the double-cab units have two. The first 25 trailers in west end single-cab units (17000/2/4 up to 17048) were fitted with de-icing equipment from new.

The first unit of D Stock was delivered on 29 June 1979 to Ruislip depot and was transferred to Ealing Common for commissioning on the same day. The commissioning of all D stock was undertaken at Ealing Common, being taken there from Ruislip between CO/CP and, later, R Stock pilot units specially adapted for the purpose. The first train of D Stock entered service on Monday 28 January 1980 and was formed of cars 7532-17532-7533 + 7528-17528-7529.

Unit 8043-17043-7043 was delivered in November 1980 fitted with Knorr-Bremse experimental braking equipment of German manufacture. Having been used on extensive tests, it entered

A double-ended unit of D Stock awaits departure from Upminster in May 2002 on a working to Richmond. Being a double-ended unit, the cab ends have inter-car-barrier fittings, necessary because the cabs may be found in the middle of trains. Brian Hardy

service in April 1981. Unit 7080-17080-8080 was delivered in October 1981 fitted with Westinghouse Analogue braking. Both have recently been scheduled for conversion to 'standard' as part of a programme of engineering modifications.

In order to assist disabled passengers, one door on each side of each car was fitted with a grab handle. All units from 7082-17082-8082 onwards were fitted with them at Metro-Cammell and those in service before unit 7082 were modified at Ealing Common. These handles had to be removed in 1990 owing to misuse by the hooligan element of society.

The interior ventilation on all Underground rolling stock has been a contentious issue probably from day one. The D Stock was no exception, originally being built with no opening windows (apart from the windows in the communicating doors). Very soon it became apparent that interior temperatures were unacceptable in warm weather. Because of that, DM 7108 of unit 7108-17108-8108 was delivered in June 1982 with experimental ventilation equipment, including grilles over the car windows, pull-down quarter lights, except at door pockets, and additional slots for expelled air on the car roof. Following the testing of this equipment it was decided that all D Stock trains should be modified similarly, but without the grilles above the windows. The prototype unit returned to Metro-Cammell in October 1982, being modified and returned with the last unit of D stock (8129-17129-7129) on 29 June 1983, exactly four years from the delivery of the very first unit. The 20 double-cab units of D Stock were modified at Acton Works between March 1983 and June 1984, whereas the single-cab units were returned to Metro-Cammell at Birmingham in pairs from March 1983, the last to be received back in modified condition being units 7080 and 7059 in January 1985. DM 7108, although now the same as all the other modified units, remains distinguishable as the prototype in that the grilles over the car windows have been panelled over.

Despite the ventilation modifications, it was still considered necessary for all train doors to be open during the warmer months

Trailer car 8008 at
Ealing Broadway.
D Stock is the only
Underground stock now
in use with single-leaf
passenger doors.
Capital Transport

and generally from May to October, all door opening was handed
back to train crews. Before OPO the guard operated the doors and
special switches were fitted for use by depot staff, who set them to
'passenger open' or 'guard's open' as appropriate. It was not surpris-
ing that these earned the nickname POGO switches and are still
referred to as such today, even though the doors are opened by the
train operator. In the last few years, however, a change to LUL safety
policy has seen 'passenger open' discontinued, not only on the
D Stock, but on all stocks so fitted. Whilst this may be of some
comfort in the summer, it has the opposite effect in the winter,
especially at terminal stations and prolonged station stops.

With service reductions having taken place on most Underground
lines from December 1982 and ventilation modifications being
completed in January 1985, there was ample spare D Stock available
to provide the service on the East London Line, allowing displaced
A60/62 Stock to form a float for OPO conversion. Double-cab units of
D Stock took over on the East London Line from 27 April 1985,
initially as crew-operated trains, but OPO from 13 May 1985. The
upturn of traffic caused subsequent need to increase the District Line
service and with the A Stock OPO conversion completed, the latter
returned to the East London Line in May 1987, the complete D Stock
fleet now operating in the District main line.

Modifications to the D Stock took place between 1994 and 1996.
Initially this comprised a number of engineering modifications, and
the only visible differences were with the train whistle which was
moved above the left front cab window and a new cab door between
the saloon and driver's cab. During these modifications, Train
Monitoring System (TMS) equipment replaced the original TEPs, and
Correct Side Door Enable equipment was fitted. All modifications
were completed by December 1996. More recently, from 2001, blue
car numbers on DM cars have been additionally positioned on the cab
front, above the nearside and offside cab windows. The same work
has seen the red numbers at the ends at waist level being removed
and larger blue numbers applied above the car windows at the ends.

Interior of refurbished trailer 17008, showing the new fittings, which include a new seating moquette and stronger armrests. At the far end to the right of the communicating door can be observed a twin transverse seat, which has replaced four longitudinal seats, the remaining space being designated for wheelchairs etc.
Les Collings

A close-up of the new seating moquette on refurbished trailer 17008 (which is now being applied to the existing unrefurbished trains). For the first time, much use has been made of green, especially in the grab rails and poles. Fred Ivey

With the D Stock midway through its operational life, early proposals for refurbishment were deferred because of financial constraints. However, in 1999, work was authorised for a trial involving one trailer car. Unit 7008 was chosen for the trial and went to Acton Works in March 1999. The interior was gutted and new fittings installed. The theme was green, akin to but not an exact shade of District Line green. At one car end, two pairs of transverse seats have been fitted with adjacent tip-up-seats, which also provides space for disabled passengers in wheelchairs. For passenger security, end

With end windows being cut into the refurbished trailer, to be of benefit, the adjacent cars were also given end windows, which will be a unique feature to the unrefurbished cars of the unit. DM 7008 in original style shows its new feature.
Daniel Woodhouse

Unrefurbished cars of D Stock are being fitted with seats covered with the new design of moquette.
Capital Transport

windows were cut into the car ends, but to be of any value, end windows were also cut into ends of the adjacent unrefurbished cars (7008 and 8008). Corporate livery was applied to all three cars of the unit by the use of vinyl.

Under the PPP contracts for the London Underground, the D Stock is to be refurbished as a matter of urgency. In the meantime, the complete D Stock fleet is receiving the new moquette as on the prototype refurbishment, which will make the original yellow/orange/brown extinct.

The vehicles of London Underground's service stock fleet are maintained by 'TransPlant' which embraces the operation of engineers trains. The mainstay of London Underground's service stock locomotives are 29 battery locomotives built between 1964 and 1974. The 13 Metro-Cammell 1964-built locomotives (L20–32) included eight for the Victoria Line, L25–32 originally having ATO equipment fitted, the others replacing steam locomotives. As with previous battery locomotives, although the bodies were built new, the traction motors,

A pair of 1973 BREL-built battery locomotives pass through Eastcote on 25 March 1998 on a transfer trip between Ruislip and Lillie Bridge depots. All eleven locomotives of this batch are now in blue livery.
Kim Rennie

During weekend track replacement projects, many engineers' trains can be found at or near to the working site. On 24 March 2002, work in the South Woodford area saw a gathering of trains in Woodford sidings. A 1969 Metro-Cammell built battery locomotive stands in the loop at Woodford, with the sidings in the background occupied by many trains.
Les Collings

The ownership of the Schoma diesel locomotives, built for the Jubilee Line Extension, passed to TransPlant in 1999. They may sometimes be seen on weekend engineering work projects. No.12 (named Melanie) stands in Woodford sidings, adjacent to the station.
Kim Rennie

The Weed Killing 1938 Tube Stock motor car pair (L150+L151) is seen Harrow-on-the-Hill on 14 May 2002.
Les Collings

bogies and compressors were acquired from withdrawn stock. A further batch of five locomotives (L15-19) was built by Metro-Cammell in 1970–71 and provided the additional locomotives needed for the construction of the original section of the Jubilee Line. An additional eleven locomotives (L44–54) were built by BREL at Doncaster in 1973–74, allowing some older machines to be withdrawn and providing new locomotives for the construction of the Heathrow extension of the Piccadilly Line. This last mentioned batch had new bogies instead of second-hand ones.

All of the locomotives described above had hinged buffers which were swung back when coupling to vehicles of tube stock height, and the design was basically unchanged (apart from minor variations) from that first used in 1938, all of which have now been withdrawn, although one (L35) has been preserved by London's Transport Museum. All locomotives have a cab at each end and are built to tube loading gauge. They are able to operate directly from current, or by battery power and are most often used to operate engineers' trains,

The three centre cars (TCC2–4) of the Tunnel Cleaning Train were purpose built at Acton Works in 1972–77. TCC3 serves as the refuse car and is seen in Ruislip Depot. David Rowe

The Tunnel Cleaning Train is, by necessity, a night owl and excursions during the day are few and far between. However, after the train was fitted with ATP equipment for working on the Central Line, it made a number of test trips and is seen at North Acton. Fred Ivey

mainly at night during non-traffic hours. Various modifications have been made to the battery locomotives in recent years, most noticeably the fitting of high-intensity headlights, replacement of the swing-back buffers by spring buffers, and the fitting of buckeye couplers. More recently, during 1995–96, 18 locomotives were fitted with ATP equipment for working on the Central Line, while all of the 1973–74 BREL locomotives have been painted blue – all others are in the standard yellow livery. Following the withdrawal of the three remaining 1951–52 Pickering-built locomotives in 1997, L50–53 of the 1973–74 batch have been re-fitted at one end with a 'Ward' coupler to operate long rail trains.

A further six locomotives (L62–67) were built by Metro-Cammell in 1985/86, which broke from the traditional design. As well as changes to the front end appearance, which incorporated a cross-walkway in front of the cab windows and a sliding side cab door, Kiepe control equipment was fitted, and buckeye coupling was provided from new. All six locomotives are currently out of service and stored in Ruislip depot, pending a decision on their future.

There are two road/rail 'Unimog' vehicles for shunting use in depots. Being of 1983 (L84) and 1986 (L85) vintage they can normally be found at Ealing Common or Lillie Bridge depots, although their use has been as diverse as on the Docklands Light Railway and for the Channel Tunnel work.

The other operative locomotives comprise two Ballast Motors and two Pilot Motor cars. The latter pair (L132–133) are the 1960 Stock pilot cars for working with the Track Recording car (which was converted by BREL at Derby from a 1973 Stock trailer in 1987). The two Ballast Motors (L150–151), both in yellow livery, are the survivors of 16 converted from withdrawn 1938 Tube Stock between 1973 and 1978. Formed into a paired unit, L150 and L151 have been specially adapted as a Weed Killing train, acquiring its present equipment from Chipman's of Horsham in 1986. There are plans to replace these by 1972 MkI Tube Stock, but authorisation is still awaited.

A total of 60 ex-BR 4-axle Turbot wagons were modified by ABB at Crewe. This included air brake modifications, fitting control wiring and complete vehicle overhaul, as well as painting into yellow livery. Being built variously by BR at Shildon and Swindon, and RFS at Doncaster between 1982 and 1988, the modified wagons were delivered to London Underground during January and February 1996. They are used to carry ballast to and from site on major track replacement operations. In 1996, three cable drum wagons were delivered, built by Bombardier, replacing the original trio of 1940 vintage.

Tamping machine TMM772 is seen between Newbury Park and Barkingside on 20 January 2002 when track replacement in the Newbury Park area was being undertaken.
Les Collings

For the construction of the Jubilee Line Extension, 15 general purpose wagons, four bogie well wagons and four 4-wheel cable drum wagons were built by Bombardier and delivered to Neasden in late-1994/early-1995. To haul these wagons, 14 diesel locomotives were built by Schoma of Germany. The 2-axle 32-tonne locomotives were built to tube loading gauge suitable for working in tube tunnels. They are fitted with normal-height buffers and drop-head buckeye couplers. Nos. 1 and 5 have been fitted with a wedgelock coupler for shunting tube stock, initially in Stratford Market depot. All 14 have been given (female) names. All the 'JLE' locomotives and wagons passed to the TransPlant fleet during 1999.

The 60 Turbot Wagons originally belonged to British Rail and were converted for LUL use in 1995. A line-up of several wagons of this type is seen on the southbound Jubilee Line at West Hampstead.
Alan Kybird

Above **Some of the 1986 Procor-built Rail Wagons have been fitted with blue side boards instead of** the usual yellow. RW821 stands in the permanent way sidings in Ruislip depot. Kim Rennie

Below LUL's two Unimog road/rail shunters are seen 'off track' on 6 October 1999, with L84 ahead of L85. The photograph was taken at Lillie Bridge. Kim Rennie

SAVED FROM SCRAP

Formerly belonging to the Science Museum, City & South London electric locomotive No.1 now resides in London's Transport Museum collection and is seen in 'The Depot' at Acton on 16 October 1999. This building is only open to the public on specific days in the year, details of which are made known in advance in the railway press. Les Collings

Another former Science Museum exhibit was Pre-1938 Tube Stock DM 3327, built in 1927 by MCCW. The tube car to the left is 1972 MkI DM 3530 and to the right the end of 'green' 1986 Tube Stock DM 16, photographed on 19 March 2000. Les Collings

London's Transport Museum

The largest and most varied collection of preserved London Underground rolling stock is owned by London's Transport Museum. Some of the collection is housed in the Museum itself at Covent Garden, London WC2, which opened to the public on 29 March 1980. Some of the exhibits were formerly on display in the London Transport Collection at Syon Park. Other rail vehicles acquired over the years could not be displayed in the central London museum and were stored at many locations. When the relatively new reconstruction workshop at the Acton Town end of Ealing Common depot was vacated by Depot Engineering Support Unit, the Museum took it over and it became the store for not only rail vehicles, but buses and many other railway artefacts.

LONDON'S TRANSPORT MUSEUM,
COVENT GARDEN, LONDON WC2

Metropolitan Railway Class A 4–4–0T steam locomotive No. 23 was built in 1866 by Beyer Peacock, later becoming service stock locomotive L45. This locomotive was withdrawn in 1948, following which it was restored to 1903 condition and eventually displayed at the Museum of British Transport at Clapham until its closure in 1972, when it moved to the LT Collection at Syon Park. The locomotive also appeared at the Underground Centenary celebrations at Neasden in May 1963.

Brill branch (Wotton Tramway) 0–4–0T steam locomotive No.807, built in 1872 by Aveling & Porter.

City & South London Railway locomotive-hauled 'padded-cell' coach No.30 built by the Ashbury Carriage & Iron Co. about 1890. This coach was displayed at the old York Railway Museum from 1938 until it closed in 1973.

Metropolitan Railway milk van No.3 built in 1896 by Birmingham. It was converted to a breakdown van by the LPTB and renumbered BDV700. It was restored to original condition for the Underground Centenary in May 1963.

Metropolitan Railway 'Ashbury' or 'Bogie' stock 2nd class coach No.400 dating from 1900 and built by the Metropolitan Railway at their Neasden Works. It was converted from steam to electric working in 1921 as a 3rd class Control Trailer, renumbered 6703 by the LPTB and reconverted in 1940 to steam stock for push-pull working on the Chesham/Chalfont shuttle service, when it was further renumbered 519. After withdrawal in 1960 it was stored at Clay Cross from 1962 and later at Preston Park, Brighton. In July 1976 the coach returned to London Transport for restoration at Ruislip depot, where work was completed in 1978.

Great Northern, Piccadilly & Brompton Railway tube motor coach No.51. Built by the Hungarian Railway Carriage & Machinery Works in Raab for the Piccadilly Line, which opened in 1906, it entered service in 1909. It was renumbered by the LER in 1926 and after withdrawal in 1929, became a Ballast Motor in the service stock fleet. However, only the rear end of the car, including to the first window, is preserved, primarily to show the 'gate' end arrangement.

Metropolitan Railway electric locomotive No.5, built by Metropolitan Vickers in 1922 and named 'John Hampden' in 1927. It was withdrawn from service in 1961 and was used as a shunting locomotive at Ealing Common depot and Acton Works until acquired initially for the London Transport Collection in Syon Park.

London Transport Q23 Stock driving motor car 4248. It was originally District Railway G Class motor coach No.644 and was built by Gloucester in 1923. It was renumbered 238 by the LER in 1928 and became 4148 in 1933. The number 4248 was applied in 1965 to avoid clashing with one of the numbers intended for the 1967 Victoria Line trailers. All G class motors were originally built with hand-operated doors and were converted to air operation between 1938 and 1940.

London Transport 1938 Tube Stock motor car 11182, built by Metro-Cammell. This car is restored in Underground train red livery with gold transfers and (dummy) passenger door control push-buttons, typically as they were in the mid-1950s.

The cab end of CP Stock DM 54235 (originally P Stock Metadyne motor coach 14235, converted and renumbered in 1963) has been converted into a simulator, giving visitors a driver's-eye view of a selection of journeys on the sub-surface routes.

LONDON'S TRANSPORT MUSEUM,
THE DEPOT, ACTON, LONDON W3

Metropolitan Railway 'Jubilee' steam stock coach dating from between 1887 and 1893 and built by Cravens of Sheffield. It is the intention that this car should be restored for eventual display.

City & South London Railway electric locomotive No.13 dating from about 1890. Originally being housed in the Science Museum as No.1, it was repainted and transferred to the LT Museum at Covent Garden in 1990 to celebrate the Centenary of the City & South London Railway but is now in 'The Depot' at Acton.

Tube sleet locomotive ESL107. This started life as two separate motor coaches, one built by Metro-Carriage, the other by Birmingham, for the Central London Railway and after withdrawal from service were converted to become a sleet locomotive in 1939. The LT numbers of ESL107 were 3944 and 3981.

Metropolitan Railway 'saloon' stock trailer/driving trailer, acquired in 1985 from the Army at Shoeburyness by the North Woolwich Old Station Museum. Following vandalism on the site, it was acquired by the Museum for eventual restoration.

City & South London Railway 4-wheeled wagon No.63. This was one of a batch of 102 such wagons ordered from Gloucester in 1921 to be used during the reconstruction of the C&SLR. The majority were disposed of after the work was complete but No.63 survived, laying derelict in London Road depot for many years.

Ultimately to create a working pre-1938 Tube Stock train, former Pilot Motor cars L131 (1934 Metro-Cammell) and L134 (1927 Metro-Carriage), along with cars 27 (1925 Metro-Carriage) and 49 (1923 Cammell Laird) from the Isle of Wight, have been set aside for this long-term restoration project.
Pilot motor cars L131 and L134 were formerly numbered 3693 and 3370 respectively, while the LT numbers of the Isle of Wight cars, which returned to London Underground in October 1990, were 5279 and 7296 respectively.

District Line Q23 motor coach 4184, built by Gloucester in 1923 as G Class motor coach No.662, renumbered 274 in 1929 and to its present number in 1934. Following withdrawal from the District Line, the car, without its compressors or traction motors, was displayed outside the GRC&W Co.'s factory in Gloucester. Following the closure of the Gloucester factory, the car was put into store and returned to Ealing Common depot on 27 February 1993.

London Transport pre-1938 Tube Stock driving motor car 3327, originally London Electric Railway tube motor coach No.297 dating from 1927. When withdrawn from service it was displayed in the Science Museum, but in 1996 ownership passed to the LT Museum.

District Line Q35 Stock trailer 08063. After withdrawal in 1972 the car was sold to the London Underground Railway Society, who restored it to 1950s condition. Ownership passed to the LT Museum in 1997.

Battery locomotive L35, of 1938 vintage and built by Gloucester, withdrawn from service in April 1992.

Q38 ex-pilot motor L127 built by Gloucester. This, along with L126, was painted back to red livery in 1990 and both were given their former numbers (4416/4417).

1938 Tube Stock 4-car unit 10012-012256-12048-11012.
This unit is formed of the remaining four cars of the 'Starlight Express', which was the last train of this stock to be withdrawn from service on the Northern Line in May 1987. Having been stored at Morden, and displayed at the depot's Open Day in November 1990, it was transferred to Cockfosters in December 1991. Refurbishment to operational condition began in 1999 and was completed at Acton Works in the autumn of 2001.

District Line unpainted aluminium R49 Stock driving motor car 22679.

1972 MkI Tube Stock DM 3530. This was withdrawn from service on the Northern Line in December 1998.

1986 Prototype Tube Stock driving motor car 16, from the 'green' train 'C' built by Metro-Cammell.

LONDON'S TRANSPORT MUSEUM – STORED

Metropolitan Railway 10-ton Ballast Wagon BW214 of 1897 origin. This was one of two wagons that survived at Neasden until acquired by the Museum in 1982. It is currently stored in Acton Works.

Q38 ex-pilot motor L126 built by Gloucester. This was painted back to red livery in 1990 and given its former number (4416). It is currently in Acton Works.

1959 Stock DM 1018, which is currently stored at DERA Shoeburyness.

1983 Batch II Tube Stock DM 3734, which represents the last of the 'conventionally built' Underground rolling stock. It is currently stored in Cockfosters depot.

Q23 DM 4184 resided for many years after withdrawal outside its maker's works – the Gloucester Railway Carriage & Wagon Co. Since 1993 it has been back with London Transport and resides in the collection at 'The Depot' at Acton. Les Collings

Right The Museum's other Q23 Stock DM is in the Covent Garden Museum and its interior with tungsten lighting makes an inviting and welcoming 'warm' appearance. Brian Hardy

Below There were only six DMs of R49 Stock. Constructed in aluminium three were unpainted, the other three painted. Unpainted 22679 is currently in 'The Depot' at Acton. Les Collings

Above Used for occasional railtours, LUL's Heritage fleet includes ex-BR coaching stock, this being DTSO 76324 of a former 4-TC unit. It is seen passing Eastcote, being hauled by Sarah Siddons at the front.
Alan Kybird

Right Also part of LUL's Heritage fleet is former BR Brake Van B955096, although it never was part of LT's miscellaneous vehicle fleet. It has been given the number B586 and is seen in Ruislip depot in December 2001.
David Rowe

London Underground Limited

Located on LUL metals are a number of ex-Underground vehicles of various vintages. In addition, 13 coaches were acquired from what were British Rail and Network SouthEast, for use on rail tours and the erstwhile 'Steam on the Met' events. Seven of the coaches were formerly in 4-TC units, the others locomotive-hauled. In addition to hired steam locomotives, former Metropolitan electric locomotive No.12 'Sarah Siddons' is also used at the rear of some special trains. The complete list of LUL owned vehicles, often referred to as the 'Heritage' fleet is listed below, none of which are included in LUL's operational fleet. The future of the ex-BR coaches is in doubt. With an even more uncertain future are the older tube cars from which, it had been hoped, to make an operative train of pre-1938 Tube Stock.

LONDON UNDERGROUND-OWNED VEHICLES

No	Details
2	DM car (ex-LT 3706) built 1934 by Metro-Cammell, ex Isle of Wight.
7	DM car (ex-LT 3209) built 1931 by Metro-Cammell, ex Isle of Wight.
L11	Double-ended ex-Acton Works shunting locomotive (ex-3080/3109) built 1931 by Metro-Cammell and converted 1964.
12	Metropolitan Railway electric locomotive, named 'Sarah Siddons' and built 1922 by Metropolitan Vickers.
44	Trailer car (ex-LT 7281) built 1923 by Cammell Laird, ex Isle of Wight.
DT81	Diesel Tender from Sentinel diesel locomotive DL81.
DT82	Diesel Tender from Sentinel diesel locomotive DL82.
L130	Ex Tube Stock pilot motor car, converted 1967, ex 3690 built 1934 by Metro-Cammell.
L135	Ex Tube Stock pilot motor car, converted 1968, ex 3701 built 1934 by Metro-Cammell.
F362	Flat wagon built 1951 by Gloucester.
F384	Flat wagon built 1965 by BR Ashford.
RW479	Rail wagon built 1950 by Gloucester.
B558	Brake van built 1935 by Hurst Nelson.
B580	Brake van built 1965 by BR Ashford, previously tube stock match wagon.
B583	Brake van built 1965 by BR Ashford, previously surface stock match wagon.
B584	Brake van built 1965 by BR Ashford, previously surface stock match wagon.
B585	Brake van built 1965 by BR Ashford, previously tube stock match wagon.
B586	Brake van built 1962 by BR Ashford, ex-BR B955096.
PC850	Ex personnel carrier converted 1966, ex 7061 built 1931 by Birmingham.
PC851	Ex personnel carrier converted 1966, ex 7063 built 1931 by Birmingham.
PC855	Ex personnel carrier converted 1966, ex 7071 built 1931 by Birmingham.
TRC912	Intended track recording car converted 1978, ex-012331 built 1938 by Birmingham.
WPW1000	Ex-diesel generator wagon, well wagon in 1976, built 1937 at Acton Works.

EX-BRITISH RAIL COACHES

No	Built	Type	Acquired
5458	1969 Derby	TSO	1995
5495	1969 Derby	TSO	1995
5497	1969 Derby	TSO	1995
* 70823	1957 Metro-Cammell	TBSK	1992
* 70824	1957 Metro-Cammell	TBSK	1992
* 70855	1952 Swindon	TFK	1992
* 71163	1954 Swindon	TFK	1992
* 76297	1955 Ashford/Eastleigh	DTSO	1992
* 76298	1957 Ashford/Eastleigh	DTSO	1992
* 76322	1955 Ashford/Eastleigh	DTSO	1992
* 76324	1957 Ashford/Eastleigh	DTSO	1992
977588	1957 Metro-Cammell	BSK	1988

* Converted to 4-TC stock at York in 1966 (71163 in 1974)

Alderney Railway Society, Channel Islands

1959 Tube Stock DMs 1044 and 1045, being cars that were painted in 'Heritage' livery in 1990. These two cars were transferred to the Alderney Railway in May 2001 and replaced 1938 Tube Stock DMs 10177 and 11177 which returned to the mainland for scrap. These had been on the Isle of Alderney since 1987.

Bluebell Railway, Sheffield Park, Sussex

Metropolitan Railway steam stock coaches 368 (1st and 3rd class coach built 1898). 387 (3rd class brake coach built 1898), 394 (3rd class coach built 1900), and 412 (1st and 3rd class coach built 1900). No. 412 was built by Cravens Ltd, Sheffield and the other three by the Ashbury Railway Carriage & Iron Co. The four coaches have a varied history. No. 387 was converted to a 3rd class electric driving motor car in 1907 and became 2761 when owned by the LPTB. No. 394 was converted to a 3rd class control trailer in 1921, becoming No. 6702 with the LPTB. Nos. 368 and 412 were converted to 1st class electric trailers in 1906 and became 9702 and 9705 respectively in LPTB ownership. The four cars were re-converted in 1940 to steam stock for push-pull working on the Chalfont/Chesham shuttle and were

The Buckinghamshire Railway Centre at Quainton Road has three cars of CO/CP Stock. CO Stock DM 53028 looks resplendent in its recently acquired coat of paint on the weekend of 25/26 May 2002.
Brian Ammann

further renumbered 512 (2761), 515 (9702), 516 (9705) and 518 (6702). They were withdrawn in 1960 and were acquired by the Bluebell Railway in 1961. The four coaches, having been out of service since 1965–66, are being restored to pre-electric condition. Nos. 387 and 394 ran again for the first time in February 1999 and in May 2002 were joined by 368. No.412 is expected to be completed in 2004.

Metropolitan Railway ballast wagon BW4 of 1897 origin, transferred from Neasden depot in June 1982.

4-wheel hopper wagons HW402 and HW433, built 1935 and 1951 respectively by Gloucester.

Buckinghamshire Railway Centre, Quainton

Metropolitan Railway Class E 0–4–4T steam locomotive No.1 built by the Metropolitan Railway at Neasden and dating from 1898, renumbered L44 in the service stock fleet by the LPTB in 1938.

London Transport service stock locomotive L99, originally GWR 0–6–0PT loco No.7715 dating from 1930. This locomotive, along with former L90 from the Birmingham Railway Museum, worked in London Transport livery in May 1993 on the 'Steam on the Met' special trains. L99 also worked the 125th anniversary specials on the District Line on 5/6 June 1993, between Ealing Broadway and West Kensington.

CP Stock DM 54233. This stock was moved to Quainton Road in October 1981 for preservation. After bomb damage during the Second World War, this car was rebuilt using part of Q38 trailer 013167, which had also suffered bomb damage. In addition, two other cars of similar stock were taken by road from Ruislip depot at the end of June 1984. These were CO DM 53028 and COP trailer 013063. This therefore makes a complete 3-car unit.

Hurst Nelson brake van B557 was acquired by the Centre on the same date as the CP Stock car mentioned above.

5-ton hand-operated crane C619, built in 1914 by Cowan Sheldon, and jib carrier J690. These vehicles were unique in being the only rail vehicles to be owned jointly by the Metropolitan and Great Central Railways. C619 and J690 were normally to be found in Harrow Goods yard. They were withdrawn in 1955 but were not taken to Quainton until May 1970.

LT flat brake wagon FB578, converted in 1950 from 4-wheeled flat wagon F327 and LT 4-wheeled flat wagon F329, built by Gloucester.

Cravens Heritage Trains owns a 3-car unit of 1960 Tube Stock and a 4-car unit of 1962 Tube Stock. The former has operated many special trips around the Underground network and on 21 September 1997 the 3-car unit is at Hammersmith on the Hammersmith & City Line.
Alan Kybird

Cobham Bus Museum, Cobham, Surrey

Cab and small section of passenger saloon of 1938 Tube Stock DM car 11242.

Colne Valley Railway, Halstead, Essex

Four wheeled hopper wagon HW421 built in 1951 by Gloucester.

Cravens Heritage Trains

1960 Tube Stock 3-car unit 3906-4927-3907 and 1962 Tube Stock 4-car unit 1506-2506-9507-1507. The 1960 Stock unit has made many trips out on the London Underground, the most famous, perhaps, being the all-night trip on the Central Line on 30 July 2000 to commemorate the centenary of the Central London Railway. The 1962 Tube Stock unit remains at Hainault with the aim of restoring that unit to operating condition in the future.

Great Eastern Traction, Hardingham, Essex

Ex-LT Sentinel diesel locomotive DL82.

Island Line (Isle of Wight)

The operational fleet of 1938 Tube Stock on the Isle of Wight has been reduced to six 2-car units, the other eight cars having been withdrawn. Four of these were scrapped in April 2000, while two remain as body spares. The two all-blue cars are awaiting disposal. More recently known as the 'Island Line' under the operational arm of South West Trains, the line was taken over by Stagecoach on 13 October 1996 for an initial four-year franchise. This was extended to expire in September 2003, from when the future of the Isle of Wight railway and its trains will have to be seriously considered.

Five out of the six operational Class 483 units of 1938 Tube Stock are in blue livery with dinosaur decals. Unit 483.006 heads a 4-car train at Ryde St John's Road on 14 August 2001. The two spare non-operational cars are still in (faded) Network SouthEast livery and are kept just north of the station. Paul Bradley

When the overhauls became due in 1998, it was expected that a livery change would also occur. This did not happen until 2000, by which time it had been decided that five out of the six units would be given a themed livery. This replaced earlier proposals to have a different livery for each. The livery chosen was all blue (with a grey roof and yellow lower half cab front) but with the addition of vinyl dinosaur decals, to recognise the Isle of Wight's reputation for dinosaur fossil discoveries and to promote a dinosaur at Sandown. Each of the five units were given appropriate names as noted below. The sixth unit (483.007 and which had formed part of the 'Starlight Express' with London Underground) was repainted into London Transport red with cream window pillars. Its re-entry into service in late-2000 was thwarted by a serious flood of Ryde depot, where four out of the six units were unserviceable. Sadly, 483.007 came off the worst and is still waiting to carry passengers in its original guise.

The Island Line rolling stock situation at 1 July 2002 was as follows:

CLASS 483 2-CAR UNITS 16

(former LUL numbers in brackets)

Unit No.	DM 'A'-end North	DM 'D'-end South	Name	DM 'A'-end North	DM 'D'-end South
	FOR SERVICE			WITHDRAWN	
483.002	122 (10221)	225 (11142)	Raptor	123 † (10116)	221 † (11184)
483.004	124 (10205)	224 (11205)	T-Rex	— * (10139)	— * (11172)
483.006	126 (10297)	226 (11297)	Terry		
483.007	127 (10291)	227 (11291)			
483.008	128 (10255)	228 (11255)	Iggy		
483.009	129 (10229)	229 (11229)	Bronti		

* Former spare cars in all-blue livery now awaiting disposal.
† Spare cars retained in Network SouthEast livery.

Isle of Wight Steam Railway, Haven Street

4-wheeled hopper wagons HW435 and HW437, built in 1965 by BR at Shildon.

Above
Nothing to do with the Island Line but on the Isle of Wight nevertheless are ex-Metropolitan Railway rigid 4-wheeled coach bodies. For many years they have been in use as beach huts at St Helens, as seen on 13 August 2001. Paul Bradley

Below
The Kent & East Sussex Railway owns District Railway coach No.100, which is a rebuild of a 1st class 4-compartment steam stock car dating from around 1865. It is seen at Tenterden as part of a vintage train special. Rob Sheen

Keighley & Worth Valley Railway, Yorkshire

Metropolitan Railway steam stock brake coach 427 (3rd class 7-compartment brake coach built as a 1st class control trailer in 1905), 465 (3rd class 9-compartment coach built 1920), and 509 (1st class 7-compartment coach built 1923). Two of these vehicles (465 and 509) are owned by the Vintage Carriages Trust and are normally on display at Ingrow Museum.

London Transport service stock locomotive L89, originally GWR 0–6–0PT loco No. 5775 dating from 1929.

Kent & East Sussex Railway

In late 1979 and early 1980, restoration was carried out on a coach now numbered as District Railway 100 – a 1st class 4-compartment steam stock car dating from around 1865. The coach body was retrieved in two halves which have been joined together and mounted on a modern underframe. Whilst the coach is thus very much a hybrid, it has been superbly restored and saw passenger service from 24 August 1980.

Two of the 'Heritage' cars of 1959 Tube Stock operate on the island of Alderney, while two other cars were acquired by the Mangapps Farm Railway in Essex, where trailer 2044 is seen on 16 July 2001. Les Collings

Mangapps Farm Railway, Burnham-on-Crouch

District Line R38 motor car 22624 (originally Q38 trailer 014178, converted 1950).

1959 Tube Stock DM car 1030 and trailer 2044, both of which were from LUL's painted 'Heritage' train.

1959 Tube Stock DM 1304 was bought privately for preservation following withdrawal in 1999, and is being restored to mid-1970s condition when it first saw service on the Northern Line. It is seen in the garden of its new owner. Mike Kelly

Museum of London

Steam Crane C621, built by Thomas Smith & Sons, 1935, second-hand ex-McAlpine in 1958.

Nene Valley Railway, Peterborough

Ex-LT Sentinel diesel locomotive DL83.

North Norfolk Railway, Sheringham

4-wheeled hopper wagons HW426 and HW429, built in 1951 by Gloucester.

Pilot Holdings, Ongar, Essex

1962 Tube Stock unit 1744-2744-9745-1745 was transferred to Ongar in August and September 2001. The purpose is currently unclear.

Rutland Railway Museum, Cottesmore

Ex-LT Sentinel diesel locomotive DL81 acquired in 1994.

Weighing machine adjustment van TV751 (ex Metropolitan Railway No.7) was disposed of by the LPTB in 1944. It was purchased in 1981 from British Steel at Kettering.

Spa Valley Railway, Tunbridge Wells, Kent

Former T Stock DMs 2758 (under restoration) and 2749 (originally 258 and 249 and latterly ESL118A/B respectively). The latter was returned to service in 1995.

Hurst Nelson brake van B560 of 1935 (this replaced B556, which was damaged by fire and has been rebuilt as a box van).

Ex-LT diesel electric crane DEC622, built 1964 by Taylor & Hubbard, and jib carrier JC689. The latter is a former 1925 vintage flat wagon, converted to a jib carrier in 1952.

Ex-LT flat wagon F397 built in 1965 by Gloucester.

Severn Valley Railway, Bridgnorth, Shropshire

London Transport service stock steam locomotive L95, originally GWR 0–6–0PT 5764 (1965 BR Shildon),
Lining Machine PTL764.

South Devon Railway, Totnes, Devon

4-wheeled hopper wagon HW418, built 1951 by Gloucester.

Southern Steam Trust, Swanage

Plasser Theurer VKR05 Tamping Machine PBT762, built in 1966.

Ex-GWR pannier tank 5764 once operated for London Transport in its service stock. It is active on the Severn Valley Railway, where it is seen on 14 April 2002 arriving at Bridgnorth. Rob Sheen

Suburban Electric Railway Association

City & South London locomotive-hauled coach bodies 135 (of 1902) and 163 (of 1907). These bodies previously belonged to the London Underground Railway Society and passed to their new owners in June 2000.

Walthamstow Museum

R49 motor car 21147. This was one of just six R49 aluminium DMs, being one of three painted.

CP Stock DM 54256 that was formerly at the North Woolwich Station Museum.

1967 Tube Stock DM 3016, which was acquired in damaged and pre-refurbished condition.

Other Stock:

Ex-GWR 0–6–0 pannier tanks that were owned by London Transport variously between 1958 and 1971 include:

L90 ex 7760 of 1930, to LT 1961
L92 ex 5786 of 1930, to LT 1958
L94 ex 7752 of 1930, to LT 1959

There are a small number of other ex-LUL vehicles in private ownership and therefore these are excluded from the lists above to respect owners' wishes for anonymity. Also a number of vehicles which have been sold for disposal by LUL and have since been refurbished for use by other operators.

As listed in the Tube Stock out of Service (page 99), a number of cars of 1959 and 1962 Stock have been reprieved from the scrapyard by being used for various engineering functions. These cars retain their passenger service car numbers.

The few remaining operative cars of 1962 Tube Stock includes two pilot units, one comprising green-painted DM 1570, which is seen passing Croxley on 7 March 2002 on the occasion of a 'turning' trip. Les Collings

Below Also operative is the 8-car train which is used each autumn for 'leaf clearing' on the Central Line. Rail Treatment Car ex-NDM 9459 is seen at Woodford on 1 December 2001. Daniel Woodhouse

Main Depots

There are nine main depots which maintain London's Underground rolling stock. The oldest are at Ealing Common, which was completed in 1905 for the electrification of the District Railway; Hammersmith, opened in 1906 for the electrification of the Hammersmith & City Line, and Golders Green, opened in 1907 for the newly-built Charing Cross, Euston & Hampstead Railway and now part of today's Northern Line. Both Hammersmith and Golders Green have access at one end only, the latter site being especially restrictive.

Northfields was built for the western Piccadilly Line extensions and was opened in 1932, and until 1964 was home to a handful of District Line trains that then operated to Hounslow West (conversely, Ealing Common depot also had a small number of Piccadilly Line trains until 1964). Neasden Works of the Metropolitan Railway was rebuilt by 1938 to become the major depot for the Metropolitan and Bakerloo lines, the latter being extended from Baker Street to Stanmore in 1939. A small 2-road steam shed was also built at the north end. In anticipation of the Central Line being extended westwards from North Acton to West Ruislip a new depot was built between Ruislip Gardens and West Ruislip. Largely completed in 1939, the Second World War delayed the completion of the project and Ruislip depot was put to other uses until 1948, including being used to store spare and withdrawn rolling stock.

Interior view of the stabling shed at White City showing the old type of conductor rails still to be found here in 2001. David Rowe

Northumberland Park was built specially for the Victoria Line and was opened in 1968. Not being near an Underground station, a staff platform was built in the depot to enable trains to convey staff to and from the main Victoria Line at Seven Sisters. Stonebridge Park opened in 1979 for the Bakerloo Line. Neasden depot was shared with the new Jubilee Line and the truncated Bakerloo Line needed its own facilities.

The main depot to serve the Jubilee Line and its eastern extension is at Stratford Market. The first train for training purposes arrived by road on 10/11 December 1996, but the depot had previously been in use for engineers' vehicles working on the JLE's construction. Several other trains arrived at Stratford Market depot by road until the connection between the old and new Jubilee Line came into use in March 1998. The 17-acre depot was built on the site of a former fruit and vegetable market and the building continued the extravagant design features adopted on the Jubilee Line Extension. The depot stands 15 metres high and is raised on steel columns and joined at roof level by an intricate steel lattice-work grid under the gently curved parallelogram-shaped roof. The main shed has eleven tracks, the remainder of the trains being stabled on outside sidings.

Subsidiary and Minor Depots

There are, in addition, a number of subsidiary and minor depots, some of which provide maintenance facilities, others being purely under-cover stabling accommodation. It is not the number of trains put into service that qualifies a depot as 'main' but the type of maintenance it undertakes. Built to a similar design and of the same period as Ealing Common and Golders Green, London Road was originally the main depot for the Bakerloo Line but is now reduced to a stabling point, with almost all of the original buildings demolished. In 2002, London Road depot became London Road 'sidings'. Opened in 1913 was the small depot at New Cross on the East London Line, provided when the East London Line was electrified. Queen's Park depot opened in 1915 when the Bakerloo was extended north from

---

Paddington. It comprises two separate buildings, at the south end a 2-road 4-train shed and a 4-road shed north of the station, through which trains for Stonebridge Park and Harrow have to pass in service on the two outer tracks, connecting at the north end with Railtrack metals. The two centre tracks are used for reversing Queen's Park terminating trains. Stabling accommodation was provided at Edgware in 1924, with the extension north from Golders Green and Hendon. The depot comprises both covered accommodation and stabling sidings. Morden depot was opened in 1926 when what is now the Northern Line was extended from Clapham Common to Morden and although regarded as a 'minor' depot, it still provides the most trains for service and has many covered roads and extensive sidings. Access is southwards beyond Morden station.

Opened in 1932 was Cockfosters depot, having access from both Oakwood and Cockfosters stations. Along with Northfields depot, opened at about the same time, it replaced the original Piccadilly Line depot at Lillie Bridge (near West Kensington) which subsequently became (and still is) the depot for engineers trains (although the heavy maintenance of engineers trains is now undertaken at Ruislip). The former LNER carriage shed at Wellington sidings was adapted to take tube stock, opening as Highgate depot in 1939. Additional sidings were built nearby at the junction of the Alexandra Palace branch (Park Junction) and were known as Highgate Wood sidings. Hainault depot was built for the (eastern) Central Line extensions, but was put to other uses during the Second World War. It was also home to over 190 cars of pre-1938 Tube Stock which had to be stored because the New Works extensions were deferred in 1940 until after the war. Hainault depot partially opened in 1947 and was in full use the following year. Access is provided at both ends, via Hainault and Grange Hill stations. Both Hainault and Ruislip depots replaced White City (formerly Wood Lane) depot on the Central Line for maintenance purposes in 1948. The old Wood Lane station layout precluded trains longer than six cars being operated on the Central Line and it was not until White City station replaced it that 7- and 8-car trains could work on the line and into the depot.

The 5-track shed at Wembley Park was rebuilt in 1954, when alterations to the track layout in the area were completed. From then it was used only by the Metropolitan Line, but previously was used by both Metropolitan and Bakerloo trains. An unsafe roof structure resulted in its closure in August 1999 and work began just over a year later to repair it. This was completed in the autumn of 2001, but the shed remains to be re-commissioned for service. On the District Line, a new depot was built east of Upminster station and opened in 1958 and at about the same time nine sidings (for thirteen trains) were opened east of Barking station. These replaced the inadequate facilities at Little Ilford depot (between East Ham and Barking) which were closed and the area used for building the new East Ham EMU depot for British Railways. The work also coincided with the complete segregation of District Line tracks from those of BR between Campbell Road Junction (east of Bow Road) and Upminster, which had become an operating headache, especially in the Barking area. Stabling accommodation was also provided on the District Line between Earl's Court and Gloucester Road with access also to and from High Street Kensington. Known as Cromwell Curve depot, there were originally 18 tracks for District Line trains and two for Circle Line trains. When the West London Air Terminal was built above the line, the number of sidings was reduced in 1957 to provide just five

6-car and two 4-car length sidings, accessible only from the line between Earl's Court and High Street Kensington, unlike the former sidings which had access to and from Gloucester Road. Only the five 6-car sidings now remain and are known as Triangle Sidings.

Sidings

There are many open-air stabling sidings, which can be summarised thus. On the Metropolitan Line, the sidings at Uxbridge were opened in 1942 for stabling both Metropolitan and Piccadilly Line trains. Piccadilly Line trains ceased stabling there after January 1991, although from the new timetable of May 2001, one train once again stables overnight at Uxbridge. Additional electrified sidings were provided at Rickmansworth south of the station in 1961 to coincide with the electrification to Amersham. On the Jubilee Line, ten sidings are provided at Stanmore, which were increased from the original seven in January 1977. On the Hammersmith & City and Circle lines, sidings are provided at Edgware Road and Farringdon. There were previously two sidings at Barbican (then called Aldersgate), one of which was decommissioned after 5-car Circle Line trains were eliminated in 1959, but the other survived in use until April 1979. Stabling sidings are provided on the District Line at Parsons Green and Ealing Broadway, both of which had some shorter roads to take uncoupled portions of trains, which practice was abandoned in 1971. Ealing Broadway no longer has any service trains stabled there and the short sidings have been removed, while one extra siding was made available at Parsons Green in December 1958. For the Piccadilly Line extensions in 1932, new sidings were built at Arnos Grove and South Harrow, the latter being on the site of the 1903 car sheds built for the District Railway electrification experiments of the time. In recent years South Harrow sidings have been used only for storing withdrawn rolling stock, although one train is scheduled to stable again overnight in the near future. The post-war Central Line extensions also gained sidings at the east end, at Woodford in 1947 and Loughton in 1948. Two more were added at the latter in 1963.

There are, in addition, pairs of sidings in tube tunnels at the end of some lines used to stable trains. These are at Elephant & Castle on the Bakerloo Line, and Brixton and Walthamstow on the Victoria Line. Until April 1989, two Victoria Line trains stabled overnight at Victoria, but no longer do so.

Closed Depots

Mention should now be made of depots that have closed. The short Northern City Line had its depot (latterly just a stabling point) at Drayton Park, which closed in 1975 when British Rail took over the line for the Great Northern inner suburban electrification. The depot buildings were subsequently demolished. In 1982, the few remaining Bakerloo Line services to and from Watford Junction were withdrawn and trains no longer stabled at Croxley Green depot as they had done from 1917. Croxley Green BR depot was subsequently closed and demolished. Highgate depot, however, eventually had better fortunes. Although rebuilt in 1970, with the general reductions in services requiring fewer trains, it closed on 25 March 1984 but has since reopened (see over). (Highgate Wood sidings had been previously closed at the end of 1982).

Expansion

The subsequent upsurge of passenger traffic and the need to provide more trains saw Highgate depot modernised and it reopened in January 1989. Two tracks were set aside until mid-1990 for the safety modifications to the 1956/59 Stock to be carried out there. In the same vein, to accommodate additional trains, two extra sidings were subsequently built at Stonebridge Park depot and four at Northumberland Park depot.

In readiness for the 1995 Tube Stock, all of the depots and stabling points of the Northern Line were reconstructed. In 1996, some tracks in Morden depot were lengthened, while at Edgware additional sidings were built on the south-east side of the station, partly on the site that was originally acquired for the aborted 1935–40 Northern Line extensions. Additional sidings have also been built at High Barnet, while Highgate depot has had its stabling roads doubled in length. Work began in 1996 on the reconstruction of Golders Green depot to adapt for new 1995 Tube Stock.

Overhauls

In the early days, the individual depots performed most of the overhaul work required on their trains. In the early-1920s, it was decided to concentrate train overhauls in one central location and Acton Works opened for this role in 1922, it being enlarged over the years. Gradually, stock from all lines was taken to Acton Works for overhaul, although for the Hampstead & City (now Northern Line) trains, it was not until 1927 that a connection was opened at King's Cross to enable Acton Works to be reached. Until the Bakerloo Line was extended to Stanmore in 1939, it too had a circuitous route – via Willesden Junction and Earl's Court. Metropolitan stock began overhauls at Acton Works after the formation of the LPTB in 1933, a task previously undertaken at Neasden Works.

Modern rolling stock design and technology has reduced the amount of maintenance work required on trains. Thus, for economic reasons, it was decided to transfer overhauls of stock back to selected depots. Acton Works, however, although a shadow of its former self, gained a new Equipment Overhaul Workshop which opened in 1989 and at the end of 1990 a new heavy repair shop was opened on the high level sidings at the Acton Town end of Ealing Common depot and was known as the Depot Engineering Support Unit (DESU). The occupancy was short-lived, for the functions carried out soon transferred back to Acton Works. London's Transport Museum then acquired the premises to store its many additional road and rail vehicles, along with much other memorabilia.

As at 1 May 2002 rolling stock overhauls were carried out at the following depots:

Depot	Stock	Line
Neasden	A60/62	Metropolitan
Northumberland Park	1967/72	Victoria
Cockfosters	1973	Piccadilly
Stonebridge Park	1972 MkII	Bakerloo

The first cycle of overhauls on District Line D Stock was completed in 1996, while the C69/77 Stock no longer has complete heavy overhauls.

Finally, mention should be made of depots that were planned for the Underground. For the Bakerloo extension from Elephant & Castle to Camberwell Green, it was proposed to build a new depot at Stanmore in the late-1940s to accommodate the extra trains that would be needed. If the early post-war proposal to quadruple the tracks between Acton Town and Hanger Lane Junction (and subsequently improve the Piccadilly Line service on the Uxbridge branch) had been adopted, a new depot near Ickenham was planned. Both were abandoned at an early stage, although a very small amount of preparatory work was done at Stanmore. For the proposed Northern Line extensions under the 1935–40 New Works Programme, a new depot was actually built at Elstree. Like Ruislip and Hainault, it was incomplete when work on the extensions were deferred and Elstree was not even rail connected at that stage. Serving as an aircraft factory during the war, the Northern Line extensions were afterwards abandoned and the depot then became Aldenham Bus Overhaul Works, although not being fully equipped until 1956. However, rationalisation of bus overhaul work saw Aldenham close in November 1985 and its ultimate demolition in 1996. The site is now a business park.

DEPOT, SIDING AND PLATFORM STOCK ALLOCATIONS

The following is correct to the timetables introduced in June 2002 (Bakerloo Line) and July 2002 (Northern and Victoria lines).

Tube lines	Main Depots	Trains	Subsidiary depots	Trains	Minor depots	Trains	Sidings or platforms	Trains	Total Trains
Bakerloo	Stonebridge Park	12	Queen's Park	7	—		London Road ‡	10	
							Elephant & Castle	3	32
Central	Ruislip	15	Hainault	29	White City	12	Loughton	10	
							Woodford	6	72
Jubilee	Stratford Market	21	Neasden	16	—		Stanmore	10	47
Northern	Golders Green	16	Morden	38	Edgware	13			
					Highgate	16	High Barnet	8	91
Piccadilly	Northfields	33	Cockfosters	34	—		Arnos Grove	6	
							South Harrow	1	
							Uxbridge	1	
							Acton Town	1	76
Victoria	Northumberland Park	33	—		—		Brixton	2	
							Walthamstow	2	37
Waterloo & City	Waterloo	3	—		—		Bank	1	4
Surface lines									
District	Ealing Common	31	Upminster	29	Hammersmith	*4	Parsons Green	*8	
							Barking	1	
							Triangle Sidings	*3	76
East London	New Cross	4	Neasden	2	—		—		6
Hammersmith & City / Circle	Hammersmith	14	—		—		Farringdon	2	
							Barking	11	
							Triangle Sidings	2	
							Edgware Road	*2	31
Metropolitan	Neasden	†28	—		—		Rickmansworth	9	
							Uxbridge	7	44

‡ London Road, formerly a 'depot' is now regarded as London Road sidings.
† Total for Neasden includes 1 x 4 for Chesham shuttle.
* Includes 10 C Stock trains operating the Edgware Road – Olympia / Wimbledon section of the District Line – 4 at Hammersmith, 3 at Triangle Sidings (Cromwell Curve) and 3 at Parsons Green.

CAR LAYOUTS

These are diagrammatic drawings only. All stock has slightly chamfered ends. Doors are officially identified by letters as shown.

Bakerloo and Victoria lines

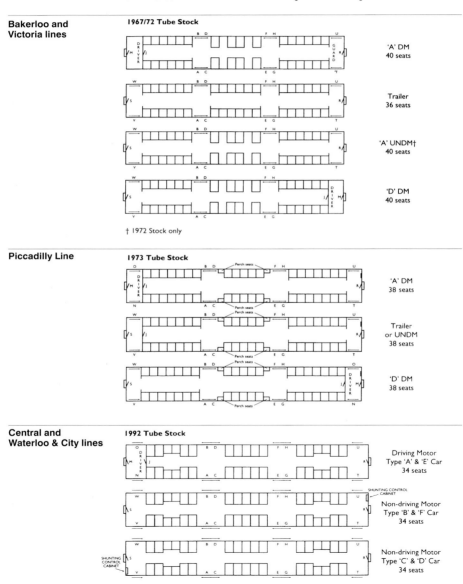

1967/72 Tube Stock

'A' DM
40 seats

Trailer
36 seats

'A' UNDM†
40 seats

'D' DM
40 seats

† 1972 Stock only

Piccadilly Line

1973 Tube Stock

'A' DM
38 seats

Trailer
or UNDM
38 seats

'D' DM
38 seats

Central and Waterloo & City lines

1992 Tube Stock

Driving Motor
Type 'A' & 'E' Car
34 seats

Non-driving Motor
Type 'B' & 'F' Car
34 seats

Non-driving Motor
Type 'C' & 'D' Car
34 seats

**Jubilee and
Northern lines**

1995 & 1996 Tube Stock

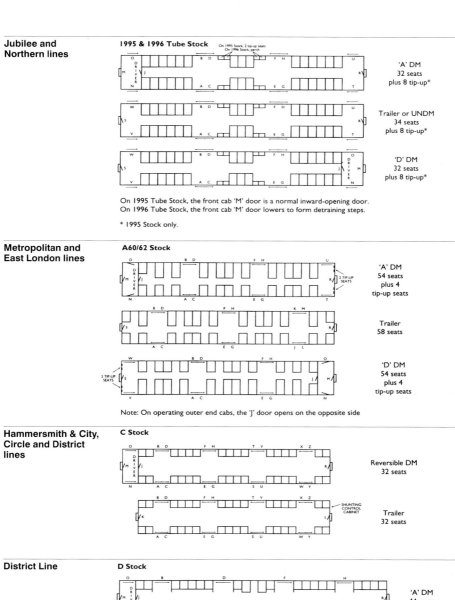

On 1995 Tube Stock, the front cab 'M' door is a normal inward-opening door.
On 1996 Tube Stock, the front cab 'M' door lowers to form detraining steps.

* 1995 Stock only.

'A' DM
32 seats
plus 8 tip-up*

Trailer or UNDM
34 seats
plus 8 tip-up*

'D' DM
32 seats
plus 8 tip-up*

**Metropolitan and
East London lines**

A60/62 Stock

'A' DM
54 seats
plus 4
tip-up seats

Trailer
58 seats

'D' DM
54 seats
plus 4
tip-up seats

Note: On operating outer end cabs, the 'J' door opens on the opposite side

**Hammersmith & City,
Circle and District
lines**

C Stock

Reversible DM
32 seats

Trailer
32 seats

District Line

D Stock

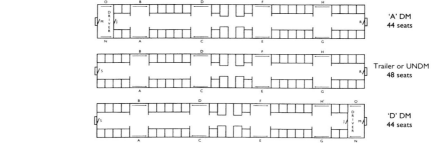

'A' DM
44 seats

Trailer or UNDM
48 seats

'D' DM
44 seats

CAR CAPACITIES

Stock	Car type	Main seats	Tip-up seats	Standing	Total
1967/72	DM	40	—	130	170
	T	36	—	156	192
	UNDM	40	—	154	194
1973	DM	38*	—	168	206
	T	38*	—	189	227
	UNDM	38*	—	189	227
1992	DM	34*	—	162	196
	NDM	34*	—	176	210
1995	DM	32	8	99	139
	T	34	8	117	159
	UNDM	34	8	117	159
1996	DM	32*	—	128	160
	T	34*	—	146	180
	UNDM	34*	—	146	180
A60/62	DM	54	4	117	171
	T	58	—	127	185
C69/77	DM	32	—	180	212
	T	32	—	180	212
D	DM	44	—	178	222
	T	48	—	184	232
	UNDM	48	—	184	232

* These cars also have 'perches' but are not regarded as proper 'seats'.

ROLLING STOCK EQUIPMENT

Stock	Traction motors	Compressors
1967	Brush LT115	Reavell TBC38Z reciprocating
1972	Brush LT115B	Reavell TBC38Z or Westinghouse 3HC43 reciprocating
1973	Brush LT118	Westinghouse 3HC43 reciprocating
1992	Brush LT130	Westinghouse V.R.S. reciprocating
1995	Frame-mounted 3-phase induction motors	Westinghouse R.S.C. rotary
1996	Frame-mounted 3-phase induction motors	Westinghouse H.R.S. reciprocating
A60	G.E.C. LT114	Westinghouse DHC5A reciprocating
A62	G.E.C. LT114	Reavell TBC38Z reciprocating
C69/77	Brush LT117	Reavell TBC38Z (all C77; some C69) or Westinghouse 3HC43 (some C69)
D	Brush LT118	Westinghouse 3HC43 reciprocating

WEIGHTS AND DIMENSIONS

Length:Length of car body, excluding couplers, etc.

Width: Maximum width of car body (on 1992/95/96 stocks, over bodyside doors).

Height: From rail level to top of car.

Dimensions are in millimetres.

Weights may vary where, for example, a car is fitted with de-icing equipment.

Stock	Car type	Weight (tonnes)	Length (mm)	Width (mm)	Height (mm)
1967	DM	30.40 *	16091	2642	2877
	T	20.30 *	15977	2642	2877
1972	DM	27.80 *	16091	2642	2877
	T	18.10 *	15977	2642	2877
	UNDM	26.50 *	15977	2642	2877
1973	DM	29.76	17475	2630	2880
	T	20.18	17475	2630	2880
	UNDM	28.53	17475	2630	2880
1992	DM	22.50	16248	2620	2869
	NDM	20.50	16248	2620	2869
1995	DM	29.40	17770	2630	2875
	T	21.50	17770	2630	2875
	UNDM	27.90	17770	2630	2875
1996	DM	29.36	17770	2630	2875
	T	20.49	17770	2630	2875
	UNDM	26.73	17770	2630	2875
A60/62	DM	31.60 *	16167	2946	3689
	T	21.50 *	16167	2946	3689
C69/77	DM	31.70 *	16030	2920	3687
	T	20.20 *	14940	2920	3687
D	DM	27.46 *	18372	2850	3620
	T	18.41 *	18119	2850	3620
	UNDM	26.12 *	18119	2850	3620

* Imperial tons

UNIT FORMATIONS

All passenger stock is formed into semi-permanent units of two, three or four cars.
These units are coupled to form trains of four, six, seven or eight cars.
On the Metropolitan (Chesham shuttle) and East London lines, single 4-car units are used.
Units/cars out of service in line unit formations are shown in italics.
Units/cars out of service and withdrawn from passenger service are shown on pages 99–101.

BAKERLOO LINE

1972 MkI & MkII Tube Stock

4-car 'A' End Units				3-car 'D' End Units			
DM 'A' End South Leading	Trailer	Trailer	DM 'D' End North Middle	UNDM 'A' End South Middle	Trailer	DM 'D' End North Leading
3231	4231	4331	3331	3431	4531	3531
3232	4232	4332	3332	3432	4532	3532
3233	4233	4333	3333	3433	4533	3533
3234	4234	4334	3334	3434	4534	3534
3235	4235	4335	3335	3435	4535	3535
3236	4236	4336	3336	3436	4536	3536
3237	4237	4337	3337	3437	4537	3537
3238	4238	4338	3338	3438	4538	3538
3239	4239	4339	3339	3440	4540	3540
3240	4240	4340	3340	3441	4541	3541
3241	4241	4341	3341	3442	4542	3542
3242	4242	4342	3342	3443	4543	3543
3243	4243	4343	3343	3444	4544	3544
3244	4244	4344	3344	3445	4545	3545
3245	4245	4345	3345	3446	4546	3546
3246	4246	4346	3346	3447	4547	3547
3247	4247	4347	3347	3448	4548	3548
3248	4248	4348	3348	3449	4549	3549
3250	4250	4350	3350	3450	4550	3550
3251	4251	4351	3351	3451	4551	3551
3252	4252	4352(d)	3352	3452	4552	3552
3253	4253	4353(d)	3353	3453	4553	3553
3254	4254	4354(d)	3354	3454	4554	3554
3255	4255	4355(d)	3355	3455	4555	3555
3256	4256	4356(d)	3356	3456	4556	3556
3258	4258	4358(d)	3358	3457	4557	3557
3259	4259	4359(d)	3359	3458	4558	3558
3260	4260	4360(d)	3360	3459	4559	3559
3261	4261	4361(d)	3361	3460	4560	3560
3262	4262	4362(d)	3362	3461	4561	3561
3263	4263	4363(d)	3363	3462	4562	3562
3264*	4264*	4364*	3364*	3463	4563	3563
3265*	4265*	4365*	3365*	3464*	4564*	3564*
3266*	4266*	4366†	3366†	3465*	4565*	3565*
3267*	4267*	4367*	3367*	3466*	4566*	3566*
				3467*	4567*	3567*

DM 'A' End South Leading	Trailer	Trailer	UNDM 'D' End North Middle
3299†	4299†	4399†	3399†

(d) Fitted with de-icing equipment.   * 1972 MkI stock cars renumbered.   † 1972 MkII stock cars renumbered.

1992 Tube Stock 2-car 'A' – 'B' Units

DM 'A' Car	NDM 'B' Car	DM 'A' Car	NDM 'B' Car	DM 'A' Car	NDM 'B' Car	DM 'A' Car	NDM 'B' Car
91001	92001	91089	92089	91177	92177	91265	92265
91003	92003	91091	92091	91179	92179	91267	92267
91005	92005	91093	92093	91181	92181	91269	92269
91007	92007	91095	92095	91183	92183	91271	92271
91009	92009	91097	92097	91185	92185	91273	92273
91011	92011	91099	92099	91187	92187	91275	92275
91013	92013	91101	92101	91189	92189	91277	92277
91015	92015	91103	92103	91191	92191	91279	92279
91017	92017	91105	92105	91193	92193	91281	92281
91019	*92019*	91107	92107	91195	92195	91283	92283
91021	92021	91109	92109	91197	92197	91285	92285
91023	92023	91111	92111	91199	92199	91287	92287
91025	92025	91113	92113	91201	92201	91289	92289
91027	92027	91115	92115	91203	92203	91291	92291
91029	92029	91117	92117	91205	92205	91293	92293
91031	92031	91119	92119	91207	92207	91295	92295
91033	92033	91121	92121	91209	92209	91297	92297
91035	92035	91123	92123	91211	92211	91299	92299
91037	92037	91125	92125	91213	92213	91301	92301
91039	92039	91127	92127	91215	92215	91303	92303
91041	92041	91129	92129	91217	92217	91305	92305
91043	92043	91131	92131	91219	92219	91307	92307
91045	*92045* ‡	91133	92133	91221	92221	*91309*	*92309*
91047	92047	91135	92135	91223	92223	91311	92311
91049	92049	91137	92137	91225	92225	91313	92313
91051	92051	91139	92139	91227	92227	91315	92315
91053	92053	91141	92141	91229	92229	91317	92317
91055	92055	91143	92143	91231	92231	91319	92319
91057	92057	91145	92145	91233	92233	91321	92321
91059	92059	91147	92147	91235	92235	91323	92323
91061	92061	91149	92149	91237	92237	91325	92325
91063	92063	91151	92151	91239	92239	91327	92327
91065	92065	91153	92153	91241	92241	91329	92329
91067	92067	91155	92155	91243	92243	91331	92331
91069	92069	91157	92157	91245	92245	91333	92333
91071	92071	91159	92159	91247	92247	91335	92335
91073	92073	91161	92161	91249	92249	91337	92337
91075	92075	91163	92163	91251	92251	91339	92339
91077	92077	91165	92165	91253	92253	91341	92341
91079	92079	91167	92167	*91255*	*92255*	91343	92343
91081	92081	91169	92169	91257	92257	91345	92345
91083	92083	91171	92171	*91259*	*92259* ‡	91347	92347
91085	92085	91173	92173	91261	92261	91349	92349
91087	92087	91175	92175	91263	92263		

‡ ATO Test Train.

CENTRAL LINE – *continued*

1992 Tube Stock 2-car 'B' – 'D' De-icing Units

NDM 'B' Car	NDM 'D' Car	NDM 'B' Car	NDM 'D' Car	NDM 'B' Car	NDM 'D' Car	NDM 'B' Car	NDM 'D' Car
92402	93402	92418	93418	92434	93434	92450	93450
92404	93404	*92420*	*93420*	92436	93436	92452	93452
92406	93406	92422	93422	92438	93438	92454	93454
92408	93408	92424	93424	92440	93440	92456	93456
92410	93410	92426	93426	*92442*	*93442* ‡§	92458	93458
92412	93412	92428	93428	92444	93444	92460	93460
92414	93414	92430	93430	92446	93446	92462	93462
92416	93416	92432	93432	92448	93448	92464	93464

1992 Tube Stock 2-car 'B' – 'C' Units

NDM 'B' Car	NDM 'C' Car	NDM 'B' Car	NDM 'C' Car	NDM 'B' Car	NDM 'C' Car	NDM 'B' Car	NDM 'C' Car
92002	93002	92070	93070	92138	93138	92206	93206
92004	93004	92072	93072	92140	93140	92208	93208
92006	93006	92074	93074	92142	93142	92210	93210
92008	93008	92076	93076	92144	93144	92212	93212
92010	93010	92078	93078	92146	93146	92214	93214
92012	93012	92080	93080	92148	93148	92216	93216
92014	93014	92082	93082	92150	93150	92218	93218
92016	93016	92084	93084	92152	93152	92220	93220
92018	*93018* ‡	92086	93086	92154	93154	92222	93222
92020	93020	92088	93088	92156	93156	92224	93224
92022	93022	92090	93090	92158	93158	92226	93226
92024	93024	92092	93092	92160	93160	92228	93228
92026	93026	92094	93094	92162	93162	92230	93230
92028	93028	92096	93096	92164	93164	92232	93232
92030	93030	92098	93098	92166	93166	92234	93234
92032	93032	92100	93100	92168	93168	92236	93236
92034	93034	92102	93102	92170	93170	92238	93238
92036	93036	92104	93104	92172	93172	92240	93240
92038	93038	92106	93106	92174	93174	92242	93242
92040	93040	92108	93108	92176	93176	92244	93244
92042	93042	92110	93110	92178	93178	92246	93246
92044	93044	92112	93112	92180	93180	92248	93248
92046	93046	92114	93114	92182	93182	92250	93250
92048	93048	92116	93116	92184	93184	92252	93252
92050	93050	92118	93118	92186	93186	92254	93254
92052	93052	92120	93120	92188	93188	92256	93256
92054	93054	92122	93122	92190	93190	92258	93258
92056	93056	92124	93124	92192	93192	92260	93260
92058	93058	92126	93126	92194	93194	92262	93262
92060	93060	92128	93128	92196	93196	92264	93264
92062	93062	92130	93130	92198	93198	92266	93266
92064	93064	92132	93132	92200	93200		
92066	93066	92134	93134	92202	93202		
92068	93068	92136	93136	92204	93204		

‡ ATO Test Train.
§ Fitted with equipment for dispensing Sandite.

WATERLOO & CITY LINE

1992 Tube Stock 2-car 'E' – 'F' Units

DM 'E' Car	NDM 'F' Car	DM 'E' Car	NDM 'F' Car	DM 'E' Car	NDM 'F' Car	DM 'E' Car	NDM 'F' Car
65501	67501	65504	67504	65507	67507	65510	67510
65502	67502	65505	67505	65508	67508		
65503	67503	65506	67506	65509	67509		

HAMMERSMITH & CITY and CIRCLE LINES and DISTRICT LINE (Edgware Road – Wimbledon)

C69 and C77 Stock 2-car Units

DM	Uncoupling Trailer	DM	Uncoupling Trailer	DM	Uncoupling Trailer	DM	Uncoupling Trailer
5501	6501	5536	6536	5571	6571	5701	6701
5502	6502	5537	6537	5572	6572	5702	6702
5503	6503	5538	6538	5573	6573	5703	6703
5504	6504	5539	6539	5574	6574	5704	6704
5505	6505	5540	6540	5575	6575	5705	6705
5506	*6506*	5541	6541	*5576*	*6576*	5706	6706
5507	6507	5542	6542	5577	6577	5707	6707
5508	6508	5543	6543(d)	5578	6578	5708	6708
5509	6509	5544	6544(d)	5579	6579	5709	6709
5510	6510	5545	6545(d)	5580	6580	5710	6710
5511	6511	5546	6546(d)	5581	6581	5711	6711
5512	6512	5547	6547(d)	5582	6582	5712	6712
5513	6513	5548	6548(d)	5583	6583	5713	6713
5514	6514	5549	6549(d)	5584	6584	5714	6714
5515	6515	5550	6550(d)	5585	6585	5715	6715
5516	6516	5551	6551(d)	5586	6586	5716	6716
5517	6517	5552	6552(d)	5587	6587	5717	6717
5518	6518	5553	6553(d)	5588	6588	5718	6718
5519	6519	5554	6554(f)	5589	6589	5719	6719
5520	6520	5555	6555(f)	5590	6590	5720	6720
5521	6521	5556	6556(f)	5591	6591	5721	6721
5522	6522	5557	6557	5592	6592	5722	6722
5523	6523	5558	6558	5593	6593	5723	6723
5524	6524	5559	6559	5594	6594	5724	6724
5525	6525	5560	6560	5595	6595	5725	6725
5526	6526	5561	6561	5596	6596	5726	6726
5527	6527	5562	6562	5597	6597	5727	6727
5528	6528	5563	6563	5598	6598	5728	6728
5529	6529	5564	6564	5599	6599	5729	6729
5530	6530	5565	6565	5600	6600	5730	6730
5531	6531	5566	6566	5601	6601	5731	6731
5532	6532	5567	6567(g)	5602	6602	5732	6732
5533	6533	5568	6568	5603	6603	5733	6733
5534	6534	5569	6569	5604	6604		
5535	6535	5570	6570	5605	6605		

(d) Fitted with de-icing equipment.
(f) Former de-icing trailer.
(g) Fitted with tinted glass windows.

DISTRICT LINE

D Stock 3-car Units
'A' Single-ended Units   ### 'D' Single-ended Units

DM 'A' End West Leading	Trailer	UNDM 'D' End East Middle	UNDM 'A' End West Middle	Trailer	DM 'D' End East Leading
7000	17000(d)	8000	8001	17001	7001
7002	17002(d)	8002	8003	17003	7003
7004	17004(d)	8004	8005	17005	7005
7006	17006(d)	8006	8007	17007	7007
7008	*17008*(d)*	*8008*	8009	17009	7009
7010	17010(d)	8010	8011	17011	7011
7012	17012(d)	8012	8013	17013	7013
7014	17014(d)	8014	8015	17015	7015
7016	17016(d)	8016	8017	17017	7017
7018	17018(d)	8018	8019	17019	7019
7020	17020(d)	8020	8021	17021	7021
7022	17022(d)	8022	8023	17023	7023
7024	17024(d)	8024	8025	17025	7025
7026	17026(d)	8026	8027	17027	7027
7028	17028(d)	8028	8029	17029	7029
7030	17030(d)	8030	8031	17031	7031
7032	17032(d)	8032	8033	17033	7033
7034	17034(d)	8034	8035	17035 †	7035
7036	17036(d)	8036	8037	17037	7037
7038	17038(d)	8038	8039	17039	7039
7040	17040(d)	8040	8041	17041	7041
7042	17042(d)	8042	8043	17043	7043
7044	17044(d)	8044	8045	17045	7045
7046	17046(d)	8046	8047	17047	7047
7048	17048(d)	8048	8049	17049	7049
7050	17050	8050	8051	17051	7051
7052	17052	8052	8053	17053	7053
7054	17054	8054	8055	17055	7055
7056	17056	8056	8057	17057	7057
7058	17058	8058	8059	17059	7059
7060	17060	8060	8061	17061	7061
7062	17062	8062	8063	17063	7063
7064	17064	8064	8065	17065	7065
7066	17066	8066	8067	17067	7067
7068	17068	8068	8069	17069	7069
7070	17070	8070	8071	17071	7071
7072	17072	8072	8073	17073	7073
7074	17074	8074	8075	17075	7075
7076	17076	8076	8077	17077 †	7077
7078	17078	8078	8079	17079	7079
7080	17080	8080	8081	17081	7081
7084	17084	8084	8085	17085	7085
7086	17086	8086	8087	17087	7087
7088	17088	8088	8089	17089	7089
7090	17090	8090	*8091*	*17091*	*7091*

DISTRICT LINE

D Stock 3-car Units – *continued*

'A' Single-ended Units   'D' Single-ended Units

DM 'A' End West Leading	Trailer	UNDM 'D' End East Middle	UNDM 'A' End West Middle	Trailer	DM 'D' End East Leading
7092	17092	8092	8093	17093	7093
7094	17094	8094	8095	17095	7095
7096	17096	8096	8097	17097	7097
7098	17098	8098	8099	17099	7099
7100	17100	8100	8101	17101	7101
7102	17102	8102	8103	17103	7103
7104	17104	8104	8105	17105	7105
7106	17106	8106	8107	17107	7107
7108	17108	8108	8109	17109	7109
7110	17110	8110	8111	17111	7111
7112	17112	8112	8113	17113	7113
7114	17114	8114	8115	17115	7115
7116	17116	8116	8117	17117	7117
7118	17118	8118	8119	17119	7119
7120	17120	8120	8121	17121	7121
7122	17122	8122	8123	17123	7123
7124	17124	8124	8125	17125	7125
7126	17126	8126	8127	17127	7127
7128	17128	8128	8129	17129	7129

(d) Fitted with de-icing equipment.

*   Prototype refurbished trailer. Whole unit in LUL corporate livery.

†   Trailers 17035 and 17077 were originally 17077 and 17035 respectively.

Unit 7080-17080-8080 fitted with Westinghouse analogue braking equipment.
To be converted to standard.
Unit 8043-17043-7043 fitted with Knorr Bremse braking equipment.
To be converted to standard.

D Stock Double-ended 3-car Units

DM 'A' End West	Trailer	DM 'D' End East	DM 'A' End West	Trailer	DM 'D' End East
7500	17500	7501	7520	17520	7521
7502	17502	7503	7522	17522	7523
7504	17504	7505	7524	17524	7525
7506	17506	7507	7526	17526	7527
7508	17508	7509	7528	17528	7529
7510	17510	7511	7530	17530	7531
7512	17512	7513	7532	17532	7533
7514	*17514*	*7515*	7534	17534	7535
7516	17516	7517	7536	17536	7537
7518	17518	7519	7538	17538	7539

JUBILEE LINE

1996 Tube Stock 3-car Units

'A' Single-ended Units   'D' Single-ended Units

DM 'A' End West Leading	Trailer	UNDM 'D' End East Middle	UNDM 'A' End West Middle	Trailer	DM 'D' End East Leading
96002	96202	96402	96401	96201	96001
96004	96204	96404	96403	96203	96003
96006	96206	96406	96405	96205	96005
96008	96208	96408	96407	96207	96007
96010	96210	96410	96409	96209	96009
96012	96212	96412	96411	96211	96011
96014	96214	96414	96413	96213	96013
96016	96216	96416	96415	96215	96015
96018	96218	96418	96417	96217	96017
96020	96220	96420	96419	96219	96019
96022	96222	96422	96421	96221	96021
96024	96224	96424	96423	96223	96023
96026	96226	96426	96425	96225	96025
96028	96228	96428	96427	96227	96027
96030	96230	96430	96429	96229	96029
96032	96232	96432	96431	96231	96031
96034	96234	96434	96433	96233	96033
96036	96236	96436	96435	96235	96035
96038	96238	96438	96437	96237	96037
96040	96240	96440	96439	96239	96039
96042	96242	96442	96441	96241	96041
96044	96244	96444	96443	96243	96043
96046	96246	96446	96445	96245	96045
96048	96248	96448	96447	96247	96047
96050	96250	96450	96449	96249	96049
96052	96252	96452	96451	96251	96051
96054	96254	96454	96453	96253	96053
96056	96256	96456	96455	96255	96055
96058	96258	96458	96457	96257	96057
96060	96260	96460	96459	96259	96059
96062	96262	96462	96461	96261	96061
96064	96264	96464	96463	96263	96063
96066	96266	96466	96465	96265	96065
96068	96268	96468	96467	96267	96067
96070	96270	96470	96469	96269	96069
96072	96272	96472	96471	96271	96071
96074	96274	96474	96473	96273	96073
96076	96276	96476	96475	96275	96075
96078	96278	96478	96477	96277	96077
96080	96880(d)	96480	96479	96279	96079
96082	96882(d)	96482	96481	96281	96081
96084	96884(d)	96484	96483	96283	96083
96086	96886(d)	96486	96485	96285	96085
96088	96888(d)	96488	96487	96287	96087
96090	96890(d)	96490	96489	96289	96089
96092	96892(d)	96492	96491	96291	96091
96094	96894(d)	96494	96493	96293	96093
96096	96896(d)	96496	96495	96295	96095
96098	96898(d)	96498	96497	96297	96097
96100	96900(d)	96500	96499	96299	96099
96102	96902(d)	96502	96501	96301	96101
96104	96904(d)	96504	96503	96303	96103
96106	96906(d)	96506	96505	96305	96105
96108	96908(d)	96508	*96507*	*96307*	*96107*
96110	96910(d)	96510	96509	96309	96109
96112	96912(d)	96512	96511	96311	96111
96114	96914(d)	96514	96513	96313	96113
96116	96916(d)	96516	96515	96315	96115
96118	96918(d)	96518	96517	96317	96117

(d) Fitted with de-icing equipment.

METROPOLITAN LINE

A60/62 Stock 4-car Units

'A' Single-ended Units

DM 'A' End North Leading	Trailer	Trailer	DM 'D' End South Middle
5000	6000(d)	6001	5001
5002	6002	6003	5003
5004	6004(d)	6005	5005
5006	6006	6007	5007
5010	6010	6011	5011
5012	6012	6013	5013
5014	6014	6015	5015
5016	6016	6017	5017
5018	6018	6019	5019
5020	6020	6021	5021
5022	6022	6023	5023
5024	6024	6025	5025
5026	6026	6027	5027
5030	6030	6031	5031
5032	6032	6033	5033
5034 *	6034	6035	5035
5038	6038	6039	5039
5040	6040	6041	5041
5042	6042	6043	5043
5044	6044	6045	5045
5046	6046	6047	5047
5048	6048	6049	5049
5050	6050	6051	5051
5052	6052	6053	5053
5054	6054	6055	5055
5068	6068	6069	5069
5070	6070	6071	5071
5072	6072	6073	5073
5074	6074	6075	5075
5076	6076	6077	5077
5078	6078	6079	5079
5080	6080	6081	5081
5082	6082	6083	5083
5084	6084	6085	5085
5086	6086	6087	5087
5124	6124	6125	5125
5126	6126	6127	5127
5128	6128	6129	5129
5130	6130	6131	5131
5132	6132	6133	5133
5134	6134	6135	5135
5136	6136	6137	5137
5138	6138	6139	5139
5142	6142	6143	5143

'D' Single-ended Units

DM 'A' End North Middle	Trailer	Trailer	DM 'D' End South Leading
5140	6140	6141	5141
5144	6144	6145	5145
5146	6146	6147	5147
5148	6148	6149	5149
5150	6150	6151	5151
5152	6152	6153	5153
5154	6154	6155	5155
5156	6156	6157	5157
5158	6158	6159	5159
5160	6160	6161	5161
5162	6162	6163	5163
5164	6164	6165	5165
5166	6166	6167	5167
5168	6168	6169	5169
5172	6172	6173	5173
5174	6174	6175	5175
5176	6176	6177	5177
5178	6178	6179	5179
5180	6180	6181	5181
5182	6182	6183	5183
5184	6184	6185	5185
5186	6186	6187	5187
5188	6188	6189	5189
5190	6190	6191	5191
5192	6192	6193	5193
5194	6194	6195	5195
5196	6196	6197	5197
5198	6198	6199	5199
5200	6200	6201	5201
5202	6202	6203	5203
5204	6204	6205	5205
5206	6206	6207	5207
5210	6210	6211	5211
5212	6212	6213	5213
5214	6214	6215	5215
5216	6216	6217	5217
5218*	6218	6219	5219
5220	6220	6221	5221
5222	6222	6223	5223
5224	6224	6225	5225
5226	6226	6227	5227
5228	6228	6229	5229
5230	6230	6231	5231

Spare trailer – 6036 (Rail Treatment Car – Sandite duties).

(d)   Fitted with de-icing equipment.
*   Cars renumbered

METROPOLITAN LINE — *continued*

A60 Stock Double-ended 4-car Units

DM 'A' End North	Trailer	Trailer	DM 'D' End South	North	DM 'A' End Trailer	Trailer	DM 'D' End South
5056	6056	6057	5057	5102	6102(d)	6103	5103
5058	6058	6059	5059	5104	6104(d)	6105	5105
5060	6060	6061	5061	5106	6106(d)	6107	5107
5062	6062	6063	5063	5108	6108(d)	6109	5109
5064	6064	6065	5065	5110	6110(d)	6111	5111
5066	6066	6067	5067	5112	6112(d)	6113	5113
5088	6088(d)	6089	5089	5114	6114(d)	6115	5115
5090	6090(d)	6091	5091	5116 *	6116(d)	6117 *	5117 *
5092	6092(d)	6093	5093	5118	6118(d)	6119	5119
5094	6094(d)	6095	5095	5120	6120(d)	6121	5121 *
5096	6096(d,g)	6097	5097	5122	6122(d)	6123	5123
5098	6098(d)	6099	5099	5232 *	6232 *	6233 *	5233 *
5100	6100(d)	6101	5101	5234 *	6234(d)*	6235 *	5235 *

* Cars renumbered
(d) Fitted with de-icing equipment
(g) Tinted glass car windows

NORTHERN LINE

1995 Tube Stock 3-car Units

DM 'D' End Leading	Trailer	UNDM 'A' End Middle	UNDM 'D' End Middle	Trailer	DM 'A' End Leading
51501	52501	53501	53502	52502	51502
51503	52503	53503	53504	52504	51504
51505	52505	53505	53506	52506	51506
51507	52507	53507	53508	52508	51508
51509	52509	53509	53510	52510	51510
51511	52511	53511	53512	52512	51512
51513	52513	53513	53514	52514	51514
51515	52515	53515	53516	52516	51516
51517	52517	53517	53518	52518	51518
51519	52519	53519	53520	52520	51520
51521	52521	53521	53522	52522	51522
51523	52523	53523	53524	52524	51524
51525	52525	53525	53526	52526	51526
51527	52527	53527	53528	52528	51528
51529	52529	53529	53530	52530	51530
51531	52531	53531	53532	52532	51532
51533	52533	53533	53534	52534	51534
51535	52535	53535	53536	52536	51536
51537	52537	53537	53538	52538	51538
51539	52539	53539	53540	52540	51540
51541	52541	53541	53542	52542	51542
51543	52543	53543	53544	52544	51544
51545	52545	53545	53546	52546	51546
51547	52547	53547	53548	52548	51548
51549	52549	53549	53550	52550	51550
51551	52551	53551	53552	52552	51552
51553	52553	53553	53554	52554	51554
51555	52555	53555	53556	52556	51556
51557	52557	53557	53558	52558	51558
51559	52559	53559	53560	52560	51560
51561	52561	53561	53562	52562	51562
51563	52563	53563	53564	52564	51564
51565	52565	53565	53566	52566	51566
51567	52567	53567	53568	52568	51568
51569	52569	53569	53570	52570	51570

1995 Tube Stock 3-car Units

DM 'D' End Leading	Trailer	UNDM 'A' End Middle	UNDM 'D' End Middle	Trailer	DM 'A' End Leading
51571	52571	53571	53572	52572	51572
51573	52573	53573	53574	52574	51574
51575	52575	53575	53576	52576	51576
51577	52577	53577	53578	52578	51578
51579	52579	53579	53580	52580	51580
51581	52581	53581	53582	52582	51582
51583	52583	53583	53584	52584	51584
51585	52585	53585	53586	52586	51586
51587	52587	53587	53588	52588	51588
51589	52589	53589	53590	52590	51590
51591	52591	53591	53592	52592	51592
51593	52593	53593	53594	52594	51594
51595	52595	53595	53596	52596	51596
51597	52597	53597	53598	52598	51598
51599	52599	53599	53600	52600	51600
51601	52601	53601	53602	52602	51602
51603	52603	53603	53604	52604	51604
51605	52605	53605	53606	52606	51606
51607	52607	53607	53608	52608	51608
51609	52609	53609	53610	52610	51610
51611	52611	53611	53612	52612	51612
51613	52613	53613	53614	52614	51614
51615	52615	53615	53616	52616	51616
51617	52617	53617	53618	52618	51618
51619	52619	53619	53620	52620	51620
51621	52621	53621	53622	52622	51622
51623	52623	53623	53624	52624	51624
51625	52625	53625	53626	52626	51626
51627	52627	53627	53628	52628	51628
51629	52629	53629	53630	52630	51630
51631	52631	53631	53632	52632	51632
51633	52633	53633	53634	52634	51634
51635	52635	53635	53636	52636	51636
51637	52637	53637	53638	52638	51638
51639	52639	53639	53640	52640	51640
51641	52641	53641	53642	52642	51642
51643	52643	53643	53644	52644	51644
51645	52645	53645	53646	52646	51646
51647	52647	53647	53648	52648	51648
51649	52649	53649	53650	52650	51650
51651	52651	53651	53652	52652	51652
51653	52653	53653	53654	52654	51654
51655	52655	53655	53656	52656	51656
51657	52657	53657	53658	52658	51658
51659	52659	53659	53660	52660	51660
51661	52661	53661	53662	52662	51662
51663	52663	53663	53664	52664	51664
51665	52665	53665	53666	52666	51666
51667	52667	53667	53668	52668	51668
51669	52669	53669	53670	52670	51670
51671	52671	53671	53672	52672	51672
51673	52673	53673	53674	52674	51674
51675	52675	53675	53676	52676	51676
51677	52677	53677	53678	52678	51678
51679	52679	53679	53680	52680	51680
51681	52681	53681	53682	52682	51682
51683	52683	53683	53684	52684	51684
51685	52685	53685	53686	52686	51686

NORTHERN LINE – *continued*
1995 Tube Stock 3-car De-icing Units

DM 'D' End Leading	Trailer	UNDM 'A' End Middle	UNDM 'D' End Middle	Trailer	DM 'A' End Leading
51701	52701	53701	53702	52702	51702
51703	52703	53703	53704	52704	51704
51705	52705	53705	53706	52706	51706
51707	52707	53707	53708	52708	51708
51709	52709	53709	53710	52710	51710
51711	52711	53711	53712	52712	51712
51713	52713	53713	53714	52714	51714
51715	52715	53715	53716	52716	51716
51717	52717	53717	53718	52718	51718
51719	52719	53719	53720	52720	51720
51721	52721	53721	53722	52722	51722
51723	52723	53723	53724	52724	51724
51725	52725	53725	53726	52726	51726

PICCADILLY LINE

1973 Tube Stock 3-car Units
'A' Single-ended Units   'D' Single-ended Units

DM 'A' End West Leading	Trailer	UNDM 'D' End East Middle	UNDM 'A' End West Middle	Trailer	DM 'D' End East Leading
100	500	300	301	501	101
102	502	302	303	503	103
104	504	304	305	505	105
106	506	306	307	507	107
108	508	308	309	509	109
110	510	310	311	511	111
112	512	312	313	513	113
116	516	316	*315*	*515*	*115*
118	518	318	317	517	117
120	520	320	319	519	119
122	522	322	321	521	121
124	524	324	323	523	123
126	526	326	325	525	125
128	528	328	327	527	127
130	530	330	329	529	129
132	532	332	331	531	131
134	534	334	333	533	133
136	536	336	335	535	135
138	538	338	337	537	137
140	540	340	339	539	139
142	542	342	341	541	141
144	544	344	343	543	143
146	546	346	345	545	145
148	548	348	347	547	147
150	550	350	349	549	149
152	552	352	351	551	151
154	554	354	353	553	153
156	556	356	355	555	155
158	558	358	357	557	157
160	560	360	359	559	159
162	562	362	361	561	161
164	564	364	363	563	163
166	566	366	365	565	165
168	568	368	367	567	167
170	570	370	369	569	169
172	572	372	371	571	171
174	574	374	373	573	173

1973 Tube Stock 3-car Units – continued

'A' Single-ended Units

DM 'A' End West Leading	Trailer	UNDM 'D' End East Middle
176	576	376
178	578	378
180	580	380
182	582	382
184	584	384
186	586	386
188	588	388
190	590	390
192	592	392
194	594	394
196	596	396
198	598	398
200	600	400
202	602	402
206	606(d)	406
208	608(d)	408
210	610(d)	410
212	612(d)	412
214	614(d)	414
216	616(d)	416
218	618(d)	418
220	620(d)	420
222	622(d)	422
224	624(d)	424
226	626(d)	426
228	628(d)	428
230	630(d)	430
232	632(d)	432
234	634(d)	434
236	636(d)	436
238	638(d)	438
240	640(d)	440
242	642(d)	442
244	644(d)	444
246	646(d)	446
248	648(d)	448
250	650(d)	450
252	652(d)	452

'D' Single-ended Units

UNDM 'A' End West Middle	Trailer	DM 'D' End East Leading
375	575	175
377	577	177
379	579	179
381	581	181
383	583	183
385	585	185
387	587	187
389	589	189
391	591	191
393	593	193
395	595	195
397	597	197
399	599	199
401	601	201
403	603	203
405	605	205
407	607	207
409	609	209
411	611	211
413	613	213
415	615	215
417	617	217
419	619	219
421	621	221
423	623	223
425	625	225
427	627	227
429	629	229
431	631	231
433	633	233
435	635	235
437	637	237
439	639	239
441	641	241
443	643	243
445	645	245
447	647	247
449	649	249
451	651	251
453	653	253

1973 Tube Stock Double-ended 3-car Units

DM 'A' End West	Trailer	DM 'D' End East	DM 'A' End West	Trailer	DM 'D' End East
854	654	855	876	676	877
856	656	857	878	678	879
858	658	859	880	680	881
860	660	861	882	682	883
862	662	863	884	684	885
864	664	865	886	686	887
866	666	867	890	690	891
868	668	869	892	692	893
870	670	871	894	694	895
872	672	873	896*	696*	897*
874	674	875			

Units 892-692-893 and 894-694-895 were formerly ETT units (Westinghouse and GEC respectively).

(d) Fitted with de-icing equipment   * Cars renumbered.

VICTORIA LINE

1967/72 Tube Stock 4-car Units

'A' Single-ended Units				'D' Single-ended Units			
DM 'A' End North Leading	Trailer	Trailer	DM 'D' End South Middle	DM 'A' End North Middle	Trailer	Trailer	DM 'D' End South Leading
3001	4001	4101 §	3101 §	3002	4002	4102	3102
3003	4003	4103 §	3103 §	3004	4004	4104	3104
3005	4005	4105 §	3105 §	3006	4006	4106	3106
3007	4007	4107 §	3107 §	3008	4008	4108	3108
3009	4009	4109	3109	3010	4010	4110	3110
3011	4011	4111	3111	3013	4013	4113	3113
3012	4012	4112	3112	3014	4014	4114	3114
3016 *	4016 *	4116 §	3116 §	3015	4015	4115	3115
3017	4017	4117	3117	3019	4019	4119	3119
3018	4018	4118	3118	3021	4021	4121	3121
3020	4020	4120	3120	3023	4023	4123	3123
3022	4022	4122 §	3122 §	3025	4025	4125	3125
3024	4024	4124	3124	3027	4027	4127	3127
3026	4026	4126	3126	3031	4031	4131	3131
3028	4028	4128	3128	3032	4032	4132	3132
3029	4029	4129	3129	3033	4033	4133	3133
3030	4030	4130	3130	3038	4038	4138	3138
3034	4034	4134	3134	3039	4039	4139	3139
3035	4035	4135	3135	3040	4040	4140	3140
3036	4036	4136	3136	3044	4044	4144	3144
3037	4037	4137	3137	3049	4049	4149	3149
3041	4041	4141 §	3141 §	3051	4051	4151	3151
3042	4042	4142	3142	3053	4053	4153	3153
3043	4043	4143	3143	3055	4055	4155	3155
3045	4045	4145	3145	3057	4057	4157	3157
3046	4046	4146	3146	3080 §	4080 §	4180 *	3180 *
3047	4047	4147	3147	3081 §	4081 §	4181 *	3181 *
3048	4048	4148	3148	3082 §	4082 §	4182 *	3182 *
3050	4050	4150	3150	3083 §	4083 §	4183 *	3183 *
3052	4052	4152 §	3152 §	3084 §	4084 §	4184 *	3184 *
3054	4054	4154	3154	3085 §	4085 §	4185 *	3185 *
3056	4056	4156	3156 §	3086 §	4086 §	4186 *	3186 *

*   1967 Tube Stock cars renumbered.
§   1972 MkI Tube Stock cars converted and renumbered to operate with 1967 Tube Stock.

1967/72 Tube Stock Double-ended 4-car Units

DM 'A' End North	Trailer	Trailer	DM 'D' End South	DM 'A' End North	Trailer	Trailer	DM 'D' End South
3058	4058	4158	3158	3069	4069	4169	3169
3059	4059	4159	3159	3070	4070	4170	3170
3060	4060	4160	3160	3071	4071	4171	3171
3061	4061	4161	3161	3072	4072	4172	3172
3062	4062	4162	3162	3073	4073	4173	3173
3063	4063	4163	3163	3074	4074	4174	3174
3064	4064	4164	3164	3075	4075	4175	3175
3065	4065	4165	3165	3076	4076	4176	3176
3066	4066	4166	3166	3077	4077	4177	3177
3067	4067	4167	3167	3078	4078	4178	3178
3068	4068	4168	3168	3079	4079	4179	3179

CARS RENUMBERED

For varied reasons, some of the rolling stock on the Underground has been renumbered. This appendix gives details of the renumbering of all current stock. For the reasons for renumbering, please refer to the appropriate chapter (for the 1962 Tube Stock see below).

1962 TUBE STOCK

Original No.	Renumbered	Date	Original No.	Renumbered	Date
2728	**2682** †	7.83	9501	**9459** ‡	5.89

† Trailer 2682 was renumbered because of the additional time needed (in 1982–84) to repair the floors of the Derby-built trailers.

‡ NDM 9459 (the Central Line 'Sandite' car) was originally renumbered 9501 in January 1983 but reverted to 9459 in March 1985. No fleet number is currently visible.

1967 TUBE STOCK

Original No.	Renumbered	Date	Original No.	Renumbered	Date
3116	**3016** *	2.95	3107	**3183**	2.89
4116	**4016** *	2.95	4107	**4183**	2.89
3101	**3180**	7.88	3122	**3186**	7.88
4101	**4180**	7.88	4122	**4186**	7.88
3103	**3181**	2.89	3156	**3184** †	5.99
4103	**4181**	2.89	4141	**4184**	10.87
3105	**3182**	7.88	3152	**3185**	5.88
4105	**4182**	7.88	4152	**4185**	5.88

* Converted from 'D'-end to 'A'-end.

† The current 3184 was converted from 1967 Tube Stock DM 3156 on date shown above. The original 3184 (ex-3141) was scrapped in July 2000.

1972 TUBE STOCK

Original No.	Renumbered	Date	Original No.	Renumbered	Date
3203	**3264**	2.92	3527	**3081** †	2.89
3204	**3116** §	2.95	3529	**3105**	2.89
3210	**3267**	6.97	4203	**4264**	2.92
3216	**3085**	5.88	4204	**4116** §	2.95
3217	**3080**	7.88	4210	**4267**	6.97
3218	**3265**	10.94	4216	**4085**	5.88
3220	**3086**	7.88	4217	**4080**	7.88
3223	**3082**	7.88	4218	**4265**	10.94
3225	**3083**	2.89	4220	**4086**	7.88
3303	**3364**	2.92	4223	**4082**	7.88
3310	**3367**	6.97	4225	**4083**	2.89
3312	**3156**	5.99	4257	**4399** §	5.99
3316	**3152**	6.88	4303	**4364**	2.92
3317	**3101**	6.88	4310	**4367**	6.97
3318	**3365**	10.94	4316	**4152**	6.88
3320	**3122**	7.88	4317	**4101**	6.88
3323	**3103**	8.88	4318	**4365**	10.94
3324	**3266** †	6.95	4320	**4122**	7.88
3325	**3107**	2.89	4323	**4103**	8.88
3349	**3366**	6.95	4324	**4266** †	6.95
3357	**3299** †	5.99	4325	**4107**	2.89
3401	**3464**	2.92	4349	**4366**	6.95
3407	**3465**	10.94	4357	**4299** †	5.99
3412	**3467**	6.97	4501	**4564**	2.92
3424	**3466**	6.95	4507	**4565**	10.94
3439	**3399** §	5.99	4512	**4567**	6.97
3501	**3564**	2.92	4516	**4141**	6.88
3507	**3565**	10.94	4520	**4084** †	10.87
3512	**3567**	6.97	4524	**4566**	6.95
3516	**3141**	6.88	4527	**4081** †	2.89

Original No.	Renumbered	Date	Original No.	Renumbered	Date
3520	3084 †	10.87	4529	4105	2.89
3524	3566	6.95			

† Converted from 'D' end to 'A' end.
§ Converted from 'A' end to 'D' end.

1973 TUBE STOCK

Original No.	Renumbered	Date
114	896	4.93
688	696	4.93
889	897	4.93

1983 TUBE STOCK

Original No.	Renumbered	Date
3728	3730	1.97

A60/62 STOCK

Original No.	Renumbered	Date	Original No.	Renumbered	Date
5008	5034	7.85	5208	5218	8.92
5009	5235	9.94	5209	5121	3.93
5028	5232	6.85	6008	6234	9.94
5034	5008 *	7.85	6009	6235	9.94
5036	5116	4.93	6028	6232	6.85
5037	5117	4.93	6037	6117	4.93
5117	5233	8.85	6117	6233	8.85

* Further renumbered 5234 in 9.94.

D STOCK

Original No.	Renumbered	Date
17035	17077	12.94
17077	17035	12.94

LONDON UNDERGROUND VEHICLES IN STOCK AS AT 1 JULY 2002

LINE SUMMARY TOTALS

Bakerloo	252
Central	680
District	450
Hammersmith/Circle	276
Jubilee	354
Metropolitan	453
Northern	636
Piccadilly	519
Victoria	344
Waterloo & City	20
Total Line	**3984**

Non-line cars

1959	3
1962	27
1972 Mk I	82
1983	90
Total Non-line	**202**

Grand Total	**4186**

STOCK SUMMARY TOTALS

1959	3
1962	27
1967	313
1972 MkI	39
1972 MkII	226
1973	519
1983 Batch I	3
1983 Batch II	87
1992	680
1992 (Waterloo & City)	20
1995	636
1996	354
Total Tube	**3007**
A60	244
A62	209
C69	210
C77	66
D	450
Total Surface	**1179**

Grand Total	**4186**

There are three groups of London Underground rolling stock which have been withdrawn from passenger service. The smallest group comprises 27 cars of 1962 Tube Stock and three cars of the slightly older 1959 Stock. Most of the former were on the Central Line and were replaced by the 1992 Stock between 1993 and 1995, while the 1959 (and some cars of 1962 Stock) were on the Northern Line and were replaced by 1995 Stock between 1998 and 2000.

'A' DM	Trailer	NDM	'D' DM	Use
1406 †	2406(d)	9125 *	1681	Central Line engineering
1532		9533		Emergency Response Unit training Acton Works
1560	2560	9561	1561	Pilot unit Ruislip
1570 ‡	2440	9441	1441	Pilot unit Ruislip
1576	2576(d)	9577	1577	Owned by TransPlant
1680	2680	9515 *	1515	Stored Ruislip depot pending disposal
1682	2682	9459 §	1407 †	Central Line engineering
1690	2690	9691 *	1691	Owned by TransPlant

*   1959 Tube Stock (all others 1962 Tube Stock)
†   Fitted with ATP equipment for operation on the Central Line.
‡   Painted in olive green livery.
§   Rail treatment (Sandite) car and painted in red/white/blue.
(d) De-icing trailer.

When the 1972 MkI Tube Stock was withdrawn, there were plans for some of it to be used on the Victoria and Waterloo & City lines. So far this has come to nothing. Some units are stored in Hainault depot as seen in April 2002. David Rowe

The 1972 MkI Tube Stock, of which there are 82 cars withdrawn and stored, originally comprised a fleet of 210 cars. However, there are 31 in service on the Victoria Line, which have augmented the 1967 Stock, and 26 on the Bakerloo Line which have augmented the 1972 MkII Stock. A total of 71 have therefore been scrapped. It was the original intention to retain and refurbish the 20 trains of 1972 MkI Tube Stock on the Northern Line and indeed three were so treated in 1993. However, the plan was overtaken by events which saw the birth of the 1995 Tube Stock. To that end, the last train of 1972 MkI Tube Stock was withdrawn on the Northern Line on 3 February 1999 (units 3227+3518). The majority of the three-car units were scrapped but most of the 4-car units were retained. It was planned that most of these would find service elsewhere in the form of enhancing services or departmental duties, but it appears that most of what were once ambitious plans have now been shelved. The use of 1972 Stock on the Waterloo & City Line will not now happen and the proposal to convert more trains for Victoria Line service has been cancelled because of the new stock that is to be built for that line. The future for the remaining cars below is thus uncertain.

'A' DM	Trailer	Trailer	'D' DM	Location
3201	4201	4301	3301	Hainault
3202 *	4202 *	4302 *	3302 *	Acton Works (Bakerloo Line spare)
3205	4205	4330	3305	Acton Works
3206	4206	4306	3306	DERA Shoeburyness (Victoria Line spare)
3208	4208	4308	3308	Hainault
3209	4209	4309	3309	DERA Shoeburyness
3211	4211	4311	3311	Hainault
3212	4212	4312	3509 ‡	Acton Works
3213	4213	4313	3313	Lillie Bridge (TransPlant)
3214	4214	4314	3314	DERA Shoeburyness (pilot unit)
3215	4215	4315	3315	Bakerloo Line
3219	4219	4319	3319	DERA Shoeburyness
3221	4221	4321	3321	DERA Shoeburyness
3222	4222	4322	3322	DERA Shoeburyness
3226	4226	4326	3326	DERA Shoeburyness
3227 †	4227 †	4327 †	3327 †	DERA Shoeburyness
3228	4207	4328	3328	DERA Shoeburyness
3229	4229	4329	3329	Aldwych for filming and training
3230	4230	4305	3330	Hainault

UNDM	Trailer	'D' DM	Location
3411	4511	3511	Hainault for scrap
3423 *	4523 *	3523 *	Acton Works (Bakerloo Line spare)

* Painted in LUL 'corporate' livery.
† Painted in 'blue doors' livery.
‡ DM from 3-car unit.

The decision to extend the Jubilee Line from Green Park to Stratford via Canary Wharf was taken in 1993 and a complete new fleet of trains was decided upon. The 1983 Stock was thus surplus to requirements and the last ran in service on 9 July 1998. All but one unit of Batch I stock was scrapped after just 14–15 years in service apart from 16 trailers that were kept, with the Batch II stock. The intention was to provide additional trains for the Piccadilly Line. That plan, too, faltered and the trailers were scrapped in 2000. In early 2002 it became clear that the Batch II stock would not be

Also withdrawn in 1997–98 was the 1983 Tube Stock, some of which had seen less than ten years in service. The Batch I stock was scrapped immediately but the Batch II units lingered on until 2002, when scrapping commenced. Plans to utilise these trains on the Piccadilly Line, in updated form, came to nothing. Uxbridge sidings was host to three 6-car trains from 1998. DM 3651 is nearest the camera in this view on 26 October 2000.
Paul Bradley

required and scrapping of these (apart from one car retained for London's Transport Museum) began in March 2002. These had been stored in spare sidings variously at Neasden, Northfields, Uxbridge, South Harrow, Upminster and Acton Works. The following cars were outstanding disposal:

'A' DM	Trailer	'D' DM	Stored Location
3630	4630(d)	3730	Cockfosters (1983 Batch I)
3631	4631(d)	3731	Northfields
3633	4633(d)	3733	Uxbridge
3634	4634(d)	3734 *	Cockfosters
3635	4635(d)	3735	Cockfosters
3636	4636	3736	South Harrow
3637	4637	3737	Acton Works
3638	4638	3738	Upminster
3639	4639	3739	South Harrow
3640	4640	3740	South Harrow
3641	4641	3741	Upminster
3643	4643	3743	Cockfosters
3644	4644	3744	Cockfosters
3645	4645	3745	South Harrow
3646	4646	3746	South Harrow
3647	4647	3747	Cockfosters
3649	4649	3749	Acton Works
3650	4650	3750	Uxbridge
3651	4651	3751	Uxbridge
3651	4652	3752	Cockfosters
3653	4653	3753	Cockfosters
3654	4654	3754	Cockfosters
3655	4655	3755	Upminster
3656	4656	3756	Cockfosters
3657	4657	3757	Uxbridge
3658	4658	3758	Uxbridge
3659	4659	3759	South Harrow
3661	4661	3761	Upminster
3662	4662	3762	Uxbridge
3663	4663	3763	Northfields

* To be retained by London's Transport Museum

Unless noted otherwise, vehicles are in yellow livery.

DIESEL LOCOMOTIVES
(built for Jubilee Line Extension construction)   14

Built 1996 by Schoma, Germany, yellow livery

No.	Name	No.	Name
1 *	Britta Lotta	8	Emma
2	Nikki	9	Debora
3 †	Claire	10	Clementine
4	Pam	11	Joan
5 *	Sophie	12	Melanie
6 †	Denise	13	Michele
7	Annemarie	14	Carol

* Fitted with Wedgelock coupler for shunting Tube Stock.
† Fitted with emergency coupler.

BATTERY LOCOMOTIVES   35

No.	Deliv.	Builder	No.	Deliv.	Builder
§ L15	1970	Metro-Cammell	†§ L44	1974	BREL Doncaster
§ L16	1970	Metro-Cammell	†§ L45	1974	BREL Doncaster
§ L17	1971	Metro-Cammell	†§ L46	1974	BREL Doncaster
§ L18	1971	Metro-Cammell	†§ L47	1974	BREL Doncaster
§ L19	1971	Metro-Cammell	†§ L48	1974	BREL Doncaster
§ L20	1964	Metro-Cammell	†§ L49	1974	BREL Doncaster
§ L21	1964	Metro-Cammell	‡†§L50	1974	BREL Doncaster
L22	1965	Metro-Cammell	‡†§L51	1974	BREL Doncaster
L23	1965	Metro-Cammell	‡†§L52	1974	BREL Doncaster
L24	1965	Metro-Cammell	‡†§L53	1974	BREL Doncaster
L25	1965	Metro-Cammell	†§ L54	1974	BREL Doncaster
L26	1965	Metro-Cammell	* L62	1985	Metro-Cammell
L27	1965	Metro-Cammell	* L63	1985	Metro-Cammell
L28	1965	Metro-Cammell	* L64	1985	Metro-Cammell
L29	1965	Metro-Cammell	* L65	1985	Metro-Cammell
L30	1965	Metro-Cammell	* L66	1986	Metro-Cammell
L31	1965	Metro-Cammell	* L67	1986	Metro-Cammell
L32	1965	Metro-Cammell			

All locomotives are fitted with emergency couplers.

* Withdrawn from service.
† Painted blue.
‡ Fitted with Ward couplers at one end only.
§ Fitted with ATP equipment.

TUBE STOCK PILOT AND BALLAST MOTOR CARS   4

No.	Origin	Converted	Previous No.	Built by	Type
§ L132	1960	1987 BREL	3901	Cravens	Pilot
§ L133	1960	1987 BREL	3905	Cravens	Pilot
L150	1938	1978 Acton	* 10327	Metro-Cammell	Weed Killer
L151	1938	1978 Acton	* 11327	Metro-Cammell	Weed Killer

* These cars were originally numbered 90327 and 91327 respectively.
§ Fitted with buckeye couplers at inner ends at 'main line' height, fitted with ATP equipment and painted in corporate livery.

BOGIE FLAT WAGONS (30 tons capacity)   3

No.	Year	Built by
F351	1951	Gloucester
F355	1951	Gloucester
F398	1965	BR Ashford

F351 and F355 operate as a permanently-coupled pair.

BOGIE HOPPER WAGONS (30 tonnes capacity)   22

Built by W.H. Davis 1981

HW201	HW205	HW209	HW213	HW217	HW221
HW202	HW206	HW210	HW214	HW218	HW222
HW203	HW207	HW211	HW215	HW219	
HW204	HW208	HW212	HW216	HW220	

FIRST GENERATION RAIL WAGONS (20 tons capacity)   9

No.	Year	Built by	No.	Year	Built by
RW490 ‡	1958	Gloucester	RW495 ‡	1965	BR Ashford
RW491	1958	Gloucester	RW499 †	1965	BR Ashford
RW492	1958	Gloucester	RW505 *	1965	BR Ashford
RW493	1958	Gloucester	RW506 *	1965	BR Ashford
RW494 †	1958	Gloucester			

   *   Wooden side boards painted blue.
   †   Fitted with winch for operating with long welded rail train.
   ‡   Fitted with chute for operating with long welded rail train.

DIESEL CRANES   6

No.	Builder	Year	No.	Builder	Year
C623 *	Cowan Sheldon	1982	DHC627 †	Cowan Sheldon	1986
C624 *	Cowan Sheldon	1984	DHC628 †	Cowan Boyd	1993
C625 *	Cowan Sheldon	1984			
C626 *	Cowan Sheldon	1984			

   *   7½-tonne crane
   †   10-tonne twin-jib crane

TRACK RECORDING CAR   1

TRC666   Converted 1987, ex-1973 Stock trailer 514.
            Fitted with buckeye couplers at 'main line' height. In corporate livery.

PLASSER-THEURER TRACK MAINTENANCE MACHINES   3

No.	Date new	Type
TMM771 *	1980	PU0716 Tamping Machine
TMM772	1980	PU0716 Tamping Machine
TMM773 †	1980	PU0716 Tamping Machine

   *   Fitted with ATP equipment for use on the Central Line.
   †   Named 'Alan Jenkins' in January 2002 after repaint. This was the first tamping
       machine (in 2002) to carry its 'TMM' prefix.

UNIMOG ROAD/RAIL VEHICLES   2

No.	Date	Reg. No.
L84	1983	A456NWX
L85	1986	C622EWT

RAIL WAGONS (20 tonnes capacity)   26

Built 1986 by Procor, fitted with buckeye couplers

RW801†	RW805	RW809	RW812	RW815	RW818‡	RW821*	RW824*
RW802†	RW806	RW810	RW813	RW816	RW819	RW822*	RW825*
RW803†	RW807	RW811	RW814	RW817	RW820	RW823*	RW826*
RW804†	RW808						

     *   Wooden side boards painted blue.
     †   Fitted with side-operated electric cranes (trade name 'ELK' equipment).
     ‡   Fitted with load winch.

HIGH-DECK WAGONS (40 tonnes capacity)   6

Built 1987 by Procor, fitted with buckeye couplers

HD871 *	HD872	HD873	HD874	HD875 *	HD876

     *   Fitted with hand-operated winch units.

GENERAL PURPOSE WAGONS (30 tonnes capacity)   41

Built 1985 by Procor

GP901	GP907	GP912	GP917	GP922	GP927	GP932	GP937
GP902	GP908	GP913	GP918	GP923	GP928	GP933	GP938
GP903	GP909	GP914	GP919	GP924	GP929	GP934	GP939
GP904	GP910	GP915	GP920	GP925	GP930	GP935	GP940
GP905	GP911	GP916	GP921	GP926	GP931	GP936	GP941
GP906							

CEMENT MIXER/MATCH WAGONS   12

Built 1987 by Procor, fitted with buckeye couplers.

Numbered CM950–955 and MW956–961, these operate as CM/MW coupled twin units in the following formations:

CM950 MW956	CM952 MW959	CM954 MW958
CM951 MW957	CM953 MW961	CM955 MW960

CABLE WELL WAGONS   3

Built 1996 by Bombardier

CW1053	CW1054	CW1055

TUNNEL CLEANING TRAIN   1

TCC1 *	Driving Motor 'A' end ex-1938 Stock DM 10226	
TCC2	Dust Extractor Car	Built 1972–77 Acton Works
TCC3	Heavy Refuse Car	Built 1972–77 Acton Works
TCC4	Dust Extractor Car	Built 1972–77 Acton Works
TCC5 *	Driving Motor 'D' end ex-1938 Stock DM 10087	

     *   Fitted with ATP equipment.

GENERAL PURPOSE WAGONS ex-Jubilee Line Extension   15

Built 1994 by Bombardier

JLE1†	JLE3*	JLE5	JLE7*	JLE9	JLE11	JLE13	JLE15
JLE2	JLE4	JLE6	JLE8	JLE10	JLE12	JLE14	

     *   JLE 3 and JLE7 permanently coupled and fitted with shingle lifting equipment.
     †   Fitted with drop-down sides.

BOGIE WELL WAGONS ex-Jubilee Line Extension   4

Built 1994 by Bombardier

JLE16   JLE17   JLE18   JLE19

4-WHEEL CABLE DRUM WAGONS ex-Jubilee Line Extension   4

Built 1994 by Bombardier

JLE20   JLE21   JLE22   JLE23

TURBOT WAGONS (34 tonnes capacity)   60

Built 1982–1988 variously by BR Shildon and Swindon, and RFS Doncaster.
Converted by ABB Crewe in 1995.
SB231–239 have 'long' drawgear, SB 240–290 'short' drawgear.

Former No.	DB No.	Former No.	DB No.	Former No.	DB No.
SB 231	978865	SB 251	978753	SB 271	978617
SB 232	978047	SB 252	978884	SB 272	978669
SB 233	978916	SB 253	978767	SB 273	978678
SB 234	978864	SB 254	978143	SB 274	978682
SB 235	978820	SB 255	978886	SB 275	978685
SB 236	978702	SB 256	978653	SB 276	978688
SB 237	978677	SB 257	978626	SB 277	978773
SB 238	987788	SB 258	978016	SB 278	978783
SB 239	978809	SB 259	978026	SB 279	978787
SB 240	978647	SB 260	978028	SB 280	978797
SB 241	978652	SB 261	978051	SB 281	978808
SB 242	978766	SB 262	978076	SB 282	978810
SB 243	978897	SB 263	978086	SB 283	978824
SB 244	978898	SB 264	978145	SB 284	978830
SB 245	978088	SB 265	978161	SB 285	978846
SB 246	978901	SB 266	978211	SB 286	978858
SB 247	978628	SB 267	978318	SB 287	978869
SB 248	978003	SB 268	978408	SB 288	978892
SB 249	978614	SB 269	978420	SB 289	978895
SB 250	978700	SB 270	978608	SB290	978918

PERMAQUIP TRACK MAINTENANCE MACHINE   1

Built 1988 by Permaquip

94801   Ex-Network SouthEast (Waterloo & City) in 1994.

Stored in Ruislip depot.

RAIL LIFTING TRANSPORTATION UNIT   1

Un-numbered, built by Bance in 1998 for the Waterloo & City Line.

DOCKLANDS LIGHT RAILWAY

Operating at 750V d.c. 3rd rail (underside contact), the initial sections of the Docklands Light Railway from Tower Gateway and Stratford to Island Gardens opened to the public on 31 August 1987, for which eleven light rail vehicles (numbered 01–11 and known as P.86 Stock) were built by Linke Hofmann Busch of Salzgitter, Germany. Each train consisted of a 2-body articulated section with accommodation for two wheelchairs. Each articulated unit had four double doorways on each side which opened and folded back inwards. The cars were finished in a red and blue livery with white bands, the red extending up and over the top of the doors. Apart from unit 07, which entered service on 2 September 1987, all vehicles entered service on the opening day, 31 August 1987.

The Docklands Light Railway operates entirely automatically, being computer controlled from the system headquarters at Poplar, where the original depot is located. On board each train is a member of staff who is able to start the train from any doorway position. In the event of a problem, manual driving is possible by using controls in a 'desk' normally locked out of use at the outer ends of the vehicles. Originally called 'Train Captains', they are now 'Passenger Service Agents'.

The P.86 Stock was not designed, nor was suitable, for tunnel running and when the initial railway was conceived, no tunnel

The DLR now has two sections of underground railway, comprising the Bank extension (opened in 1991) and between Mudchute and Greenwich under the River Thames. B.92 Stock vehicle 62 stands at Island Gardens on its way to Lewisham.
Capital Transport

routes were planned. However, the proposal to extend the railway into the City, to provide a quick and direct link into the fast growing Canary Wharf complex, construction of an extension from Royal Mint Street (east of Tower Gateway) to Bank commenced in March 1988. This was in twin tube tunnels for most of the way, save for a steep open-air ramp from the existing line to connect with the tunnels. For passenger services to Bank, a second batch of ten vehicles (P.89 Stock) was built by BREL of York. Numbered 12 to 21, these ten units were delivered to Poplar between December 1989 and May 1990. Unit 12 was the first to enter service on 11th May 1990, supplementing the original trains and enabling increased services to operate. The P.89 Stock cars when new were very similar to their older P.86 counterparts and although only a small number of minor detail differences exist between them, the P.89 Stock was built to operate in tunnel conditions.

In addition to providing an extension to Bank, it was also desirable to operate two-unit trains whenever possible and with a further extension from Poplar east to Beckton given the go-ahead, more new stock was required. A total of 70 articulated units were ordered from BN Constructions Ferrovaires et Metalliques of Bruges in Belgium. The first batch, known as B.90 Stock and fitted with the then existing signalling equipment, comprised 23 vehicles (22–44). The B Stock trains differed from their P Stock sisters by having sliding doors mounted outside the car body and having a redesigned front end with centre access. There were 66 seats per vehicle (plus four tip-up seats), but with more longitudinal seating than with the P type.

The first B.90 unit (22) arrived on 31 January 1991 and entered service on 1 July 1991. The extension to Bank was opened on 29 July 1991, at first using the westbound tunnel only, but double-line operation commenced on 29 November 1991. The B.90 Stock thus complemented the existing vehicles to provide the service between

By 1 July 2002, four of the new B.92 trains built in 2001–2 by BN (92, 93, 95 and 96) had entered service. Although there are several cosmetic differences between the new vehicles and the older ones, the most noticeable is that the passenger doors are painted white. Vehicle 96 arrives at Crossharbour & London Arena on 12 July 2002. Brian Hardy

from Bank, Tower Gateway and Stratford to Island Gardens. The P.86 trains were banned from running to Bank and always worked singly, but 2-unit operation (of both P.89 and B.90 types, but never mixed) commenced from 25 February 1991, although rather spasmodically to start with.

The remainder of the B Stock fleet (47 vehicles numbered 45–91) was classed as B.92 Stock and from new was fitted with Alcatel signalling equipment, although in other respects they are identical in appearance to the B.90 stock. One of the B.90 Stock cars (35) was delivered in August 1991 fitted with Alcatel signalling for test purposes, along with the first two B.92 units (45–46) in October 1991. The remainder of the B.92 Stock was delivered direct to the new Beckton depot between March 1992 and March 1993. Opening of the Beckton extension was achieved on 28 March 1994, initially as a shuttle service to and from Poplar, with through services to Tower Gateway from 31 July 1995.

Cosmetic changes to DLR rolling stock saw LT-style 'Light Rail' roundels applied from June 1991, indicating LRT's ownership of the system, but with the transfer of control from LRT to the LDDC on 1 April 1992, these were hastily removed in March 1992. The cars then continued with their original signing and numbers until March 1993, when a new Docklands 'Light Rail' logo was introduced. In November 1995 B.92 unit 45 appeared in service in corporate DLR livery of petrol blue and grey, being a trial with self-adhesive vinyl film over the original colours. This lasted until the autumn of 1998 when, along with vehicle 74, an all-over-advertisement livery for the London Knights Ice Hockey Team was launched. Since then a number of other DLR trains have received advertisement liveries and to date a total of 16 vehicles are in all-over-advert liveries, summarised as follows:

22	Serco Docklands	50	Golden Jubilee
34	Greenwich Maritime	51	Diet Coke
35	Greenwich Maritime	56	Serco Docklands
45	London Knights Ice Hockey	66	Trend Microsystems
46	Lewisham Shopping Centre	67	Jaguar Cars
47	Lewisham Shopping Centre	68	Jaguar Cars
48	Diet Coke	74	London Knights Ice Hockey
49	Golden Jubilee	91	Trend Microsystems

B.92 (converted ex-B.90) unit 32 has had an interior modernisation in 1996 to generate more standing space, at the expense of ten seats in each centre bay. Subsequent to this experiment, and because of the higher than anticipated ridership, a total of 20 vehicles were modified to provide more standing space at the expense of 20 seats per vehicle. The vehicles converted were 45 and 50–67, along with further modifications to the prototype No.32.

Construction began in September 1996 of a further extension of the DLR, to take the southern leg in tunnel under the River Thames to terminate at Lewisham. This opened on 20 November 1999 with two new 'underground' stations. That at Island Gardens was built by the cut-and-cover method and is close to the surface, but Cutty Sark (which did not open until 3 December 1999) is deep below the surface with two pairs of escalators linking platform level with the surface.

The new Alcatel signalling system was introduced on the DLR in stages, first on the Beckton extension, followed by Stratford – Canary Wharf on 18 April 1995, and the rest of the railway on 10 July 1995.

From this latter date, the P.89 and remaining P.86 units became superfluous, being unable to operate on the new system. Whilst the B.90 cars have subsequently been converted to match their B.92 counterparts, the P.86 cars were purchased by Essen Verkehrs AG (EVAG) in Germany, back in 1991. Between 1991 and 1995, the cars made their way back to Germany to their new owners. The same company also purchased the P.89 cars in 1996 and during 1996 and 1997 these cars were shipped onwards to Germany.

Another extension to the Docklands Light Railway is planned, to serve London City Airport, with the possibility of an under-river projection to Woolwich. For the Airport link and enhanced services in the future, 24 vehicles of the B.92 type are being built by BN in Bruges. With only the numbers 01–21 vacant, it was decided to continue on at the end of the existing B.92 stock and then start again at 01. The new stock is thus being numbered 01–16 and 92–99, with those in the '9x' series being delivered first. They are almost identical to their B.92 counterparts (and are indeed classified as B.92 stock), apart from white-painted passenger doors. The first new train to arrive at Beckton was in fact 93 on 17 January 2002. As at 1 July 2002, nine had been delivered with in four service.

Rolling Stock as at 1 July 2002 was as follows:

B.90 STOCK (BN) – CONVERTED EX-B.90   23

Built by BN, Bruges, Belgium, 1991 and converted to B.92 Stock 1993–98.

22	23	24	25	26	27	28	29	30	31
32*	33	34	35†	36	37	38	39	40	41
42	43	44							

B.92 STOCK (BN)   47

Built by BN, Bruges, Belgium 1991–93.

45*	46	47	48	49	50*	51*	52*	53*	54*
55*	56*	57*	58*	59*	60*	61*	62*	63*	64*
65*	66*	67*	68	69	70	71	72	73	74
75	76	77	78	79	80	81	82	83	84
85	86	87	88	89	90	91			

B.92 STOCK (BN)   24

Built by BN, Bruges, Belgium 2001–2002.
Note that vehicles 92–99 and 01 had been delivered by 1 July 2002.
Delivery of the other vehicles will be completed during 2002.

01	02	03	04	05	06	07	08	09	10
11	12	13	14	15	16	92	93	94	95
96	97	98	99						

   * Reduced interior seating with more standing space 1997-98.
   † B.92 prototype unit.

WORKS VEHICLES   9

Vehicle	Number	Vehicle	Number
Ballast Hopper	990	Flat Wagon	996
CT30 Crane	992	Freightliner Flat	997
Battery Locomotive	993	Freightliner 3-Plank	998
GEC Diesel	994	Freightliner Flat	999
Ruston Diesel	995		

992–999 were previously 92–99 and 990 was previously 100.

POST OFFICE RAILWAY

Construction of the Post Office Tube railway was begun in 1915, but because of the First World War it was another 12 years before the first section was opened. This was on 5 December 1927 between Paddington and Mount Pleasant, the next section opening on eastwards to Liverpool Street on 28 December 1927. The final section to Eastern District Office at Whitechapel opened on 2 January 1928. This non-passenger carrying railway at first conveyed only parcels until 13 February 1928, from when letters were carried as well. The railway is 6.44 miles in length and the 2ft gauge tracks are generally in double-track tube tunnels of 9ft diameter, separating at station approaches into single tube tunnels of 7ft diameter. The driverless trains operate on a centre 3rd rail system at either 150V d.c. in station areas, or at 440V d.c. between stations, allowing speeds of about 7mph and 35mph respectively. The automatic operation of the trains is controlled by track circuits. One of the running rails is bonded to earth and acts as a common return for both traction and track circuiting. The other rail is, electrically, a series of individual lengths insulated from each other. When the wheels of a train bridge the rails, the relay connected to that particular track circuit operates, removing power from the preceding section and not restoring it until the train has moved onto the next section. The train brakes operate in the absence of traction current and thus the system is fail-safe. At stations, train movements were controlled manually from a switch frame, which was mechanically and electrically interlocked. Trains

The mainstay of Mail Rail are the 34 trains built by Greenbat in 1980–82. Car 503 (now 03) is stabled between duties at Mount Pleasant. Brian Hardy

No.36 (ex-756) is one of the 1930–31 English Electric trains and is seen in the depot at Mount Pleasant, minus its containers.
Brian Hardy

could thus be shunted or manually routed through. A new computerised signalling system was installed on the railway, replacing the manually-operated switch cabins at stations. Commissioned in station-by-station stages from east to west from 13th June 1993, the last stage was completed on 25th July 1993 at Paddington.

Because of the opening of the new Willesden Distribution Centre, which handles most of the mail in the London area, the role of the Post Office railway has declined. Reductions in services from 30 September 1996 resulted in the railway operating for 18 hours a day, from 13.00 to 07.00, the six hour break being utilised for maintenance purposes. Major engineering and maintenance work is undertaken when the line closes at 07.00 on Saturday until 13.00 Monday. Just four operational stations remain – Paddington, Rathbone Place, Mount Pleasant and Whitechapel Eastern District office. One or two units per train operate according to traffic requirements and the normal 5-minute interval service is supplemented with additional trains as traffic demands. The trains are serviced and maintained at the depot at Mount Pleasant, which is connected to the main running lines by a steeply graded incline.

For the opening of the railway, 90 4-wheel cars were built by the Kilmarnock Engineering Company with equipment by English Electric, and were designed to operate in 3-vehicle formation. These cars were not successful and were replaced between 1930 and 1931 by 50 bogie cars from English Electric, being numbered 752–763 and 793–830, the first entering service singly in May 1930. Two-car operation with these new cars commenced on 9 September 1930. A further ten similar cars (923–932) were delivered in 1936 because of increasing postal traffic. These 60 cars thus provided the daily service very reliably over the next 45 years or more. The mail containers, however, originally built of plywood, were replaced by aluminium containers in the 1950s following experiments in 1948.

Two prototype trains were built by English Electric in 1962, entering service in 1964. No further examples were built and one was scrapped in 1973, the other being withdrawn in 1980. To replace the bulk of the 1930–36 stock, 34 new cars numbered 501–534 were built by Greenbat of Leeds and were delivered to the railway at Mount Pleasant between 1980 and 1982. In addition, two end bogies were provided as spares (both numbered 535) to replace fellow motor ends when necessary. From the outset the new cars were painted in Post Office red, unlike their predecessors, which were in pale green. Two cars, however (801 and 806), were repainted into 'gold' livery in 1977 to celebrate the railway's Golden Jubilee.

In addition to the 34 new Greenbat cars, 17 of the 1930–36 type were retained, refurbished and subsequently returned to service in 1985–86. These were repainted in Post Office red to match the Greenbat cars. Three of these cars have been converted with a new design of ramp lowering device, of the type fitted to the Greenbat cars. The remaining 1962 prototype was also returned to service in 1986 by salvaging equipment from the previously withdrawn pair, bearing the fleet number 66.

In 1987, two of the Greenbat cars (514 and 532) were fitted with new canopies, giving a completely new look. Both have now reverted to standard.

To enable the trains to be compatible with the new system, all operational trains (apart from prototype car 66) were renumbered from the end of September 1992. Former numbers are shown in the list below. The old 1930–36 Stock cars stored at various locations, and the spare Greenbat bogies, have not been renumbered. In addition, the fleet of 1930–36 cars has been reduced by two, to 15.

1980 GREENBAT — 35

01 (501)	02 (502)	03 (503)	04 (504)	05 (505)	06 (506)	07 (507)
08 (508)	09 (509)	10 (510)	11 (511)	12 (512)	13 (513)	14 (514)
15 (515)	16 (516)	17 (517)	18 (518)	19 (519)	20 (520)	21 (521)
22 (522)	23 (523)	24 (524)	25 (525)	26 (526)	27 (527)	28 (528)
29 (529)	30 (530)	31 (531)	32 (532)	33 (533)	34 (534)	† 535

† 535 comprises two single motor bogies.

1930–31 ENGLISH ELECTRIC — 13

35 (755)	36 (756)	37 (760)	38 (761)	39 (762)	*41 (805)	42 (806)
43 (811)	44 (812)	45 (814)	47 (819)	48 (824)	49 (827)	

* 805 body ex-817 in 1981.

1936 ENGLISH ELECTRIC — 2

50 (928)	51 (931)

SPECIAL DUTY (VIP) CAR 1   PERSONNEL CARRIER 1

753	821

1926 BATTERY CARS — 3

1	2	3

CARS STORED OUT OF SERVICE — 23

66	752	759	763	793	795	797	799	802	804
810	813	816	817	818	820	822	826	828	830
925	930	932							

The following cars are preserved:

601:	Mount Pleasant Workshop – 1927 4-wheeled stock.
803:	Buckinghamshire Railway Centre, Quainton Road – 1930/31 English Electric.
807:	Science Museum – 1930/31 English Electric.
808:	West Somerset Railway, Minehead – 1930/31 English Electric.
809:	National Railway Museum, York – 1930/31 English Electric.